SALVATION MADE SURE,

OR,

AN ATTEMPT TO SHOW

THAT ALL CHRISTIANS DO NOT OBTAIN THE FULL ASSURANCE OF HOPE; THAT ALL CHRISTIANS CAN OBTAIN IT; THE WAY TO OBTAIN IT; AND THE IMPORTANCE OF OBTAINING IT.

WITH

AN APPENDIX,

CONTAINING

SOME REMARKS ON THE NATURE OF SPIRITUAL DARKNESS; TOGETHER WITH SOME DIRECTIONS TO THOSE WHO ARE LABORING UNDER IT.

BY

REV. WILLIAM BACON.

SEVENTH EDITION.

AUBURN:
WILLIAM J. MOSES.
1856.

PREFACE TO THE SEVENTH EDITION.

It is now thirty years since this little volume was first published. Former editions of it were recommended by Rev. Doctors Matthew, L. R. Perrine, formerly Professor in the Theological Seminary at Auburn, N. Y.; Henry R. Weed, of Wheeling, Va.; and President Thomas J. Briggs, of Cincinnati, Ohio; and the Author has had the satisfaction of learning from many, that they had been happily relieved from their doubts and distresses, by perusing it. But for reasons, the relation of which would pain the writer more than it would profit his readers, the book has been for several years out of print; and it is now reprinted at the earnest request of many. The errors which are opposed in the first and second chapters may not be as prevalent now as when the book was written; but it is believed that the matter contained in the third and fourth chapters, and the Appendix, is as needful as ever. Again, therefore, the little book is sent forth, with prayer for its usefulness.

PREFACE.

Before my entrance into the ministry of the Gospel, I was called by a particular providence of God, to search out non-professing Christians. My observations while thus occupied, convinced me that such an employment was not a little needed, and might be not a little useful to the cause of Christ. And early in my ministry I was called to labour as a missionary, in places where no churches were organized. This led me again to hunt up hidden saints. In this employment my former impressions were much confirmed. And by all my subsequent observations I have been more and more convinced, that there are more non-professing Christians in our several congregations, than is generally supposed; and that the duty of searching them out is very much neglected by those who have the care of souls. Now the most of these persons keep from professing religion through fear that they are not Christians. They therefore need assistance to obtain a good hope. But it has appeared to me, that many who labour for the spiritual welfare of their fellow men, have thought themselves bound to aid them in every other concern, except that of gaining evidence of their own salvation: or rather that their only duty in this respect, was to guard inquirers against ill-founded hopes: and that if any would have "a good hope through grace," they must find their way to it through all possible difficulties, unaided by the instructions of others. Nay I fear that in some instances they have acted from the mistaken notion, that the only way to keep inquirers from a *false* hope, is to increase the difficulty of gaining a *genuine* one.

In refusing to assist others in obtaining "a good hope through grace," these persons are probably actuated by a fear lest they shall encourage those to hope who have no ground to hope. And in general it would be unsafe to tell a man they believed him a Christian, even if they had good evidence. But this is not necessary. All they have to do is to tell him what are evidences of grace and what are not; and then leave him to judge for himself whether, he has these evidences or not. They may assure him with the utmost confidence, that *if he have such and such exercises of heart* he is a Christian, and do it with the utmost safety; for at the same time, they can guard him against deception by cautioning him not to think he has these evidences when he has them not.

On this subject I was once perplexed. I dared not to give instruction lest I should give dangerous encouragement. But upon farther consideration, I concluded that it was safe to *tell the truth:* and since then, I have never feared to tell the inquirer what were Scripture evidences of saving grace, and to urge him no longer to disbelieve them to be such Nay, I hesitate not to insist, that he shall either believe himself a Christian, or conclude that he has none of those exercises of heart which the Scriptures declare to be evidences of saving grace. And yet I find room enough for caution. I tell him the heart is deceitful: that the great danger lies in thinking he has these exercises while he has them not. And such is the course which I have endeavoured to take in the following work.

Observation has also taught me, that by far the greater part of *hoping* and professing Christians are troubled with many doubts and fears: and that these their doubts and ears are not only a great affliction to themselves; but (by checking their growth in grace, and preventing their activity in religion) they are a great detriment to the cause of Christ. Theirs is, then, a case which demands attention: and yet, so far as my observations have extended; it is a case which has hitherto been very much neglected by those who should watch for souls.

And so far as I have been able to ascertain the causes of the doubts and fears which perplex Christians, they have been mostly occasioned by ignorance or error, respecting the real evidences of a saving change of heart: or, from the mistaken notion, that they must of necessity remain in this uncertainty; by which opinion they have been discouraged from striving "to make their calling and election sure." Their case calls loudly, therefore, for instruction on this important subject.

The present is an age of peculiar exertion, light and prosperity in the cause of Christ. Unusual exertions are made to carry the Gospel to the heathen. Many classes of sinners in Christian lands hitherto neglected, are now receiving special attention from the people of God. Numerous new ways of doing good have been devised. Every department of the church seems to have additional attention paid to it. Almost every doctrine and duty is illustrated with greater clearness, and urged with greater force. And by the special outpourings of his Spirit, God is giving signal success to these exertions: thus rapidly extending and perfecting his church. But while all this is done, the subject of *the Christian's hope* is comparatively neglected. And yet the extension of the Redeemer's kingdom, by bringing more to be concerned in it, has given this subject additional importance.

These considerations led me to think that something like what is here attempted, was greatly needed. Much, it is true, may be done by the Pastor in his public and private instructions. But it will be impossible for him to *time* his instructions to the occasional doubts and fears of his parishioners; nor can their difficulties be so well removed by public instruction from the pulpit, as from perusing a treatise on the subject in the closet. In some instances the pastor might afford them instruction in conversation. But this would be such a tax upon his time, as must keep him from other important duties of his office. How much better would it be for *him*, and for *them*, if he could cite them to a treatise on the subject, in which they could find all the instruction that they needed. They could then sit down at leisure for alternate instruction and self-examination.

On the subject of 'the Full Assurance of Hope,' much, it is true, has hitherto been written. But it has been published generally in connexion with other subjects; and in works too dear to be generally purchased, and too voluminous to be generally read. To meet the exigence of the case there needs a separate work on the subject, *so cheap that all can buy it, so concise that all can read it.* This demand is intended to be met in the present work. I pretend not so much to teach what is new, as to select, arrange in a judicious order, and thus embody in one work, what others have previously published. Many thoughts, however, which I have not seen in other authors, I have ventured to insert; and hope they may not be useless to the reader.

The subject of 'Spiritual Darkness' is very seldom treated on, either from the pulpit or the press; and yet there occasionally occur some most distressing cases of it. It therefore demands attention. And it was this consideration which led to the *Remarks* and *Directions* contained in the Appendix. I appended them to the treatise on the Full Assurance of Hope, because the subjects are somewhat related; and because it was not expedient to publish them in a separate work.

In this little work, *usefulness* not literary merit, has been my aim. I have not written for the learned and refined, much less for the fastidious: but for plain, unlettered and honest inquirers after the evidences of saving grace. To them, I have therefore endeavoured to accommodate my language and style. My studied simplicity and plainness may seem to many the result of faulty negligence. But I only regret that I have not been more simple and plain.

With these prefatory remarks, this little work is committed to the public with more solicitude for its usefulness than for its reputation.

INTRODUCTION.

The subject upon which it is proposed to treat in the following pages, is of the utmost importance to every individual. Every individual should therefore give it his first and chief attention. As the reader sits down then, to the perusal of this work, let him reflect that the subject of it involves his highest interest; and therefore demands his most prayerful and earnest attention: that however imperfectly the work itself may be executed, it still is of no little importance to him, because of the momentous concern of which it treats. Imperfect as this work may be, a candid and prayerful perusal of it might lead some fearful and desponding saint to a cheerful and animating assurance of eternal life. It might also convince some self-deceived sinner, that while he has been so confident that he stood firm on the Rock of ages, he has been ready to sink amidst the billows of the wrath of God. And thus it might be the means of leading him to seek and to obtain deliverance from hell, and admission into heaven. Let the reader sit down to this work, then, with deep interest and fervent prayer.

For the successful investigation of any subject, it is important that we have a clear and definite idea what that subject is. And as many have somewhat vague and indistinct ideas of the one before us, it may not be amiss to give it a brief explanation.

Our subject is, SALVATION MADE SURE. What then is Salvation? and what is it *to make* that salvation *sure?* In its most extensive import, Salvation signifies *deliverance from danger.* But in a gospel sense, it signifies *deliverance from the practice and punishment of sin:* from the practice of it by sanctification; and from the punishment of it by justification. Sanctification is a progressive work. It is begun in regeneration, and is not completed until death. But justification is an instantaneous and a perfect work. By this act of God's grace, the sinner is at once set free from all the punishment of sin.

But gospel salvation includes something more than deliverance from sin and its punishment. It confers a consequent gracious claim to eternal happiness. It not only delivers from hell, but conducts to heaven. Justification *admits* the sinner to heaven. Sanctification *prepares* him for its duties and enjoyments. This salvation is granted to the sinner for the sake of that atonement which Christ has made for sin in "his obedience unto death." It is offered to the sinner on condition, that he exercises a certain kind of *faith*, called in Scripture; "faith in Christ," "faith in his blood," "the faith which worketh by love," and "the faith of God's elect." This faith has its seat in the *heart*, and not in the understanding merely. "With the *heart man believeth* unto righteousness." Rom. x. 10. Faith is not a notion of the mind, but a temper and action of the soul. It is an earnest and confiding application of the heart to God for salvation through the atonement of Christ. This prepares us for our next inquiry.

What is it then, *to make this* salvation *sure?* It is made sure *in fact* and *in event*, by the exercise of the faith above described. For it is the promise of "God who cannot lie," that "He that believeth—shall be saved." If, then, the sinner but exercises this faith, he cannot fail of salvation. The thing *in itself* is perfectly sure, even though the sinner himself may not be aware of it.

But it is not this abstract and absolute certainty of salvation, this "objective assurance," as Flavel calls it, concerning which we propose to treat. But it is that certainty which is apprehended and felt by the believing sinner himself, called by the same author, "subjective or personal assurance." To make his salvation sure in this sense, he must not only exercise saving faith, but gain assurance that he has exercised it. This assurance is founded on certain evidences. To make our salvation sure, then, is to gain full and sufficient evidence that we have saving faith.

The assurance of salvation now under consideration, is called in Scripture, "the full assurance of hope." Heb. vi. 11. Many confound this with "the full assurance of *faith*," spoken of in Heb. x. 22. Hence they often speak of "the faith of assurance." But the one is very different from the other. "Full assurance of *faith*" is an undoubting belief of what God has revealed in his word, especially perhaps what he has promised in the Gospel. "The full assurance of *hope*" is an entire confidence that we have complied with the condition on which salvation is offered, and that we shall therefore assuredly be saved. The former is *general*, having regard to all that God has revealed: the latter is *particular* and *personal*, having regard only to our own salvation. Faith goes before hope. Faith, that is, *saving* faith, is the foundation on which hope rests; for we hope we shall be saved, because we have previously exercised this particular faith. The assurance of the one, then, must be very different from the assurance of the other.

Some confound 'assurance of hope" with *perfection in holiness:* insisting that they are the same, or at least that the one implies the other. But they are altogether different in their natures; nor have they scarcely any relation with each other. It is true, the more faithful we are in duty, the more evidence there is that we shall be saved. But all this evidence may not be *seen* by us. And the assurance is not measured by the amount of evidence *existing*, but by the amount of evidence *discovered*. The degree of our assurance does not depend entirely on the degree of our faithfulness in duty. It depends also, on our faithfulness in self-examination. Perfection in duty, then, is no way necessary to the full assurance of hope.

What is now to be said on the subject of making our salvation sure, is upon the supposition that the doctrine of Saint's

Perseverance is true. If, however, any reader doubts this doctrine, he can regard what is said as relating, not to the evidence that we shall finally be saved, but to the evidence that we have been born again.

Many insist that the full assurance of hope is necessarily attained by all real Christians; that no man can possibly be born again without this assurance. Others go to the opposite extreme, and insist that *none* can have it. The sentiment to be maintained, is the one that lies between these two extremes. It is not true that Christians must necessarily know that they are Christians. Neither is it true that none can know that they are Christians. It is true that although many real Christians do not have the full assurance of hope, yet it is possible for all of them to have it.

It is proposed to show in this work,

I. That the opinion that all Christians *must of necessity* have the full assurance of hope, is *false and dangerous*. But,

II. That all Christians *may* and *ought* to gain this full assurance of hope.

III. How it is to be obtained. And

IV. That it is vastly important that it should be obtained

SALVATION MADE SURE.

CHAPTER I.

THE OPINION THAT ALL SAINTS MUST OF NECESSITY HAVE FULL ASSURANCE OF HOPE, SHOWN TO BE FALSE AND DANGEROUS.

OF those who hold this error there are two classes. The one insist that saving faith consists in believing *Christ is ours*, that he died with a view to save us in particular, and consequently that we shall assuredly receive the benefit of his death in the pardon of our sins, the sanctification of our natures, and the final salvation of our souls. The other class though they do not consider assurance of salvation as making any part of saving faith, insist nevertheless that it is inseparable from it: that is, they insist that the change of heart which takes place at the time of receiving salvation by faith, is so great and perceptible that none can experience it without knowing it. That saving faith consists 'in believing Christ is ours, and that we shall therefore assuredly be saved,' is most evidently false; for it amounts to this: 'we shall be saved, because we believe we shall be saved'—'we are Christians for we think we are Christians.' And if it be true that believing ourselves Christians makes us Christians, then there is no such thing as self-deception in regard to salvation. But how many do we see, who are altogether confident that they are real saints, while they give evidence to all around that they "have neither part nor lot in this matter." Nay, how often do the Scriptures speak of persons as having false hopes, 'thinking they stand, while ready to fall,' (1 Cor. x. 12.)—'thinking themselves something while they are nothing,' thus deceiving themselves, (Gal. vi. 3.) —'coming in to the wedding without a wedding garment,' (Matt. xxii. 11, 12.)—'having a religion which is vain,' (James i. 26.)—'coming and crying at last,' "Lord, Lord, have we not prophesied in thy name? and in thy name have cast out devils; and in thy name done many wonderful works;" but to whom Christ will say "I *never* knew you, depart from me, ye that work iniquity." Matt. vii. 22, 23. What but self-deceivers were the five foolish virgins of whom Christ spoke? And what but self-deceivers were the stony-ground hearers, who received the word *with joy;* but who endured but for a time, because they had not the root of grace in their hearts? Matt. xiii. 20, 21. But none of these things could be, if *believing* Christ ours, *made* him ours.

There is no intimation in Scripture that this *appropriating faith*, as it is called, is saving faith. It was not believing Christ to be his, that secured to Peter the divine benediction. Matt. xvi. 15—18. Nor was it this which qualified the eunuch for Christian baptism. Acts viii. 37. Faith is, indeed, the receiving of Christ, John i. 12.—Col. ii. 6. But it is not a belief that we *have* received him. Much less is it a belief that he died for us, in a higher sense than for all mankind.

Faith and hope are essentially distinct from each other. Hence they are spoken of in Scripture, as things of different import. See 1 Cor. xiii.

13. Gal. v. 5. Eph. iv. 4, 5, and Tit. i. 1, 2. The one is evidence of the other. Heb. xi. 1. The fact that we have faith is the testimony on which our hope rests. But the *proof* and *the thing proven* are entirely distinct. Hope then, and especially full assurance of hope, makes no part of saving faith.

Equally groundless is the opinion, that the change of heart which takes place on our exercising saving faith, is so evident, that we cannot experience this change without knowing it. Our charity must be very circumscribed if we do not believe this opinion to be contradicted by constant facts. We see multitudes of professors *daily*, who relate a good Christian experience, who talk and act, as if they lived in the constant exercise and enjoyment of religion, and who manifest as much constancy and faithfulness in the cause of Christ, as many who pretend to know that they are Christians; but who say nevertheless, that they are troubled with continual doubts and fears, whether they were ever born again. Must we, then, conclude, against all the evidence which they give us to the contrary, that they are yet in the gall of bitterness and bonds of iniquity? Can we be so uncharitable as to pronounce by far the greater portion of professors in the several Christian denominations to be self-deceivers or hypocrites, because they do not *know* that they are Christians?

If I mistake not, this opinion is contradicted by the experience of some of its own advocates. I think I have known some that hold to this opinion, who, on meeting with a change of heart, doubted

2

for a while whether the change had taken place, but afterwards concluded that it really had; and who therefore believe their hearts were changed before they knew that they were changed. And if they were correct in this conclusion, their own experience shows them that they can be converted without certainly knowing it.

The change which takes place at the time when the sinner receives salvation, is, it is granted, a great change. But the manifestation of that change is not so sudden and striking in some as in others. However instantaneous the change in itself must be, in some cases it unfolds itself so gradually, that the subject of it is never able to state at what precise time it took place. In many instances, this change is preceded by comparatively little opposition and distress, and is followed by comparatively little joy and zeal. And this renders the change much less plain and palpable. And when the change is visible and striking, the renewed sinner may not be aware of the nature of it. He may know, indeed, that *some* change has taken place; and yet not know that it is that *saving* change which the Scriptures denominate regeneration. Of this change he can have no correct ideas before he experiences it; for it is one of those "things of the Spirit" that must be "spiritually discerned." 1 Cor. ii. 14. Every new born soul is astonished to find what vague and incorrect notions he had formed of the new birth. Nor are we to suppose that one whose conceptions of spiritual things have been hitherto so gross and erroneous, should invariably come into right apprehensions of them at the very first moment that his spiritual sight is restored. No wonder if at the first look he "sees men as trees walking." Mark viii. 24. That when the change first takes place he should not fully understand it. Spiritual things are so subtle and complex, and the understanding even of the renewed sinner is so dull and beclouded, that it is no easy thing for him fully and immediately to comprehend them. Especially is it no easy thing for him so fully to understand the workings of his own heart, as absolutely to know that he does exercise saving faith with all its attendant graces. For "the heart is deceitful above all things, and desperately wicked: who can know it?" Jer. xvii. 9.

Moreover, the Scriptures tell us that all the Christian graces have their counterfeits: that there is not only a saving, living, active faith; but a dead, speculative faith, (James ii.)—that there is not only a 'godly sorrow which worketh repentance unto salvation;' but a 'sorrow of the world which worketh death,' (2 Cor. vii. 10.)—that there is not only a love which is evidence of a change of heart, (1 John iv. 7.) but a love which the unrenewed sinner often exercises, (Luke vi. 32.)—that there is not only a 'joy in the Holy Ghost,' and a 'joy of faith,' (Rom. xiv. 17.—Phil. i. 25.)—but a joy of the self-deceived, stony-ground hearers. Matt. xiii. 20, 21. The Scriptures tell us that many have been deceived in these respects, as was shown when speaking on the error of 'appropriating faith.' Yea, the Scriptures warn us against such deception. Is it any wise strange then, that the Christian should be afraid when the Scriptures tell him there is so much danger?

In attempting to prove that all Christians must know that they are Christians, it is said, "The state of sin and condemnation is called imprisonment, disease and death; while salvation is called release from imprisonment, restoration from sickness, yea, resurrection from the dead. And what! shall a man be delivered from a prison, from a dungeon, and not know it? Shall he be relieved from painful and wasting sickness, and not know it? Shall he even be raised from the dead, and not know it?" But these figures were used by inspiration to represent not how *plain* and *perceptible* is the evil of sin and the release from it; but how *great* and *important* they are. And many things may be very great, and yet not be very easily seen and understood. So it is emphatically with sin. Generally speaking, the more sin a man commits, the less he sees his sinfulness. When a man is in prison, or on a bed of pain, he knows it, he feels it; and when he is released from it, he readily feels and knows that he is released. But the bondage and disease of sin are not so perceptible. The ignorance of sinners respecting them is proverbial. Release from them must therefore partake in a measure of this obscurity. When released from the prison-house of sin, he knows not whether he has indeed escaped from it, or has only exchanged its inner ward for one of its outer apartments. Or the affair may appear so strange and mysterious to him, that like Peter, in his literal release from prison, he may suppose it all a vision, a dream.

In reasoning from the figurative expressions used in Scripture, we must keep close to the object for which they were used by the sacred writers themselves. When the inspired penmen introduced a figure to express one quality of a subject, it is very unsafe for us to infer from the nature of the figure itself, that this subject possesses another and different quality. For instance, to express his majesty and glory, God is called a SUN; to express the greatness of his wrath, he is called a FIRE; and to express his wisdom and knowledge, he is called LIGHT. But how erroneous would it be to infer that because these are visible things, therefore God is a visible Being? To express his sovereignty, he is called a POTTER; to express his terrible majesty, he is called a LION; and to express the power and stability of his grace, he is called a ROCK. But how unsafe would it be to infer that because these are created and perishable things, God is not self-existent and eternal. So when release from imprisonment, restoration to health, and resurrection from death are used in Scripture to express the greatness of a change of heart, it is altogether unsafe to infer from them that this change is so plain and palpable, that none can experience such a change without certainly knowing it.

Some are accustomed to speak of a *hope* with no little contempt. They seem to think the professor who only hopes and does not *know* that he is a Christian, is a fair object for ridicule. But in God's word, it is considered in a far different light. The Scriptures tell us of 'a hope in God's mercy,'

(Ps. xxxiii. 18.)—'a hope in God,' (Ps. xxxix. 7.) —'a hope in Christ,' [1 Cor. xv. 19.]—'a hope of salvation,' [1 Thess. v. 8.]—'a good hope through grace,' [2 Thess. ii. 16.]—'a hope of eternal life,' [Tit. i. 2.]—'a lively hope.' 1 Pet. i. 3. And a multitude of other expressions might be quoted, to show that a hope of salvation is no contemptible thing, at least in the view of inspiration. Indeed, the apostle exhorts believers to "*hope* to the end for the grace that is to be brought unto them at the revelation of Jesus Christ." 1 Pet. i. 13. And the Psalmist, sensible of his lack of this grace, reproves himself for it, and exhorts himself to the exercise of more hope; saying, "Why art thou cast down, O my soul? and why art thou disquieted within me? *Hope* thou in God; for I shall yet praise him for the help of his countenance." Ps. xlii. 5.

The declaration of the apostle in Rom. xiv. 23, passes very currently among many as a proof that all Christians must *know* that they are Christians. The declaration is, "He that doubteth is damned.' Doubteth what? Not whether he is a Christian as these persons suppose. Look to the chapter containing this passage, and you will see the apos le is speaking of the eating of certain meats: and the doubt of which he speaks is in relation to the propriety of eating them. It has, therefore, no relation to our hope of salvation. Besides, the apostle does not declare a man damned in consideration of his *doubting*, but of his *eating*. He says, "He that doubteth is damned *if he eat*." Furthermore, "doubt," according to the original, may mean to *distinguish*, or put a difference, that is between different kinds of meats. And this passage probably has allusion to certain meats that were forbidden in the Ceremonial law. The meaning of the passage would then be, ' He who thinks that the same distinction between clean and unclean meats, which the ceremonial law points out, ought still to be observed, " is damned ;" [that is, is condemned, is to blame for eating those kinds of meats which that law forbade.'] This passage, then, has not the least relation to our knowing that we are Christians.

There are several passages of Scripture, it is true, which prove that saints of old did have the full assurance of hope. But they prove not that *all* saints possessed it. On the contrary, it appears that some did not have it, but "through fear of death were all their lifetime subject to bondage." Heb. ii. 15. Nor do these passages prove that even those, who had full assurance, invariably possessed it from the very moment when they passed from death unto life. On the contrary, it seems that even Paul, who, at the close of his ministry, could say, "I have finished my course, I have kept the faith; henceforth there is laid up for me a crown of righteousness which the Lord, the righteous Judge, shall give me in that day," [2 Tim. iv. 7, 8.]- even this same apostle was at a previous season, afraid 'lest after preaching to others he himself should be a castaway.' 1 Cor. ix. 27. These passages are then far from proving that all saints must know from the very moment in which it takes place, that they have met with a saving change. They prove, indeed, that assurance is attainable and will therefore be considered in their proper place. But on the present point they have no bearing.

The opinion that Christians cannot but know that they have met with a change of heart, appears most evidently false, from the circumstance that the Scriptures reprove saints for not knowing it. If no saint could help knowing it, none could remain ignorant of it; consequently none could be subject to reproof for delinquency. But as some were subject to reproof of this kind, some could and did fail of knowing that they had passed from death unto life. When James and John proposed to call down fire from heaven upon the inhabitants of a certain Samaritan village; because they did not receive Christ with proper hospitality, "he turned and rebuked them, and said; ye know not what manner of spirit ye are of." Luke ix. 55. It will not be doubted by the reader that these disciples were real saints; and yet they were rebuked for not knowing what manner of spirit they were of. It may be said, indeed, that the spirit of which Christ spoke, was the temper by which they were actuated in the single concern of calling down fire upon these villagers. But this was a mistake in relation to the heart. And if they could be mistaken in this case, they might in others. They evidently supposed themselves actuated by a very great and laudable zeal for Christ in this affair; and yet they were mistaken in the moral character of that zeal. Their zeal was sinful, while they thought it holy. And if they could be thus mistaken with regard to their zeal in this instance, might they not be mistaken in relation to *all* their zeal,—supposing they had true Christian zeal for God, while they had that 'zeal of God which is not according to knowledge?' Rom. x. 2. And if they might be mistaken in relation to their zeal, might they not be mistaken in relation to faith—supposing it was a *saving*, while it was only a dead faith? So also in relation to humility, love, joy, and every other Christian affection. And if it was possible for these disciples to be thus deceived, it is possible for others also. It is not true, then, that all Christians must infallibly know that they are Christians.

Again, said the apostle to the Corinthians, "Know ye not your own selves, how that Jesus Christ is in you, except ye be reprobates?" 2 Cor. xiii. 5. To have 'Jesus Christ in us,' is to have 'Christ formed in us;' that is to be regenerated. Reprobates are those that are *not accepted;* that is, those whom God does not own as his saints. The apostle asks the Corinthians in this passage, then, if they did not know whether they were Christians or not? And this question is not an *inquiry* but a *reproof;*—and this reproof was given not to sinners, but to saints; for the epistle which contains it, was written "unto the *church* of God which is at Corinth, with all the saints which are in all Achaia." 1 ch. 1 v. Saints, then, are reproved for not having full assurance of hope. But they would not be reproved by an inspired apostle, if they were not destitute of it. All saints, there fore, do not have the full assurance of hope.

This opinion is proven false by the fact that the Scriptures call upon Christians to exert themselves to obtain the full assurance of hope. Says the apostle, [Gal. vi. 3, 4.] "For if a man think himself to be something, when he is nothing, he deceiveth himself. But let every man prove his own work, and then shall he have rejoicing in himself alone and not in another."

Evidently, to be 'something,' means to have grace, or to be a Christian;—and to be 'nothing,' means to have no grace, or to be a sinner. Here, then, the apostle suggests to the Galatians the danger of being deceived in respect to their own salvation. And against this danger he warns them, when he tells them to 'prove their own works.' He tells them to prove their own works, that they may not think themselves something while they are nothing,—to prove these works to know whether they are the works of a Christian or of a sinner. And *proof,* as used in Scripture, signifies an exertion to gain evidence. Here, then, the apostle calls on the saints at Galatia, to make some exertion to gain the full assurance of hope. But this he would not have done, if no saint could be destitute of this assurance.

Says the same apostle, [2 Cor. xiii. 5.] 'Examine yourselves whether ye be in the faith: prove your own selves.' Here the apostle calls on the Corinthian Christians to examine, to see whether they had saving faith. But examination is wholly unnecessary if saints cannot help knowing that they have faith. He calls on them to *prove,* that is, to gain proof to themselves that they had faith. But this exertion is altogether useless, if none can have faith without knowing it.

Says another apostle (2 Pet. i. 10.) "Wherefore the rather, brethren, give diligence to make your calling and election sure." This is spoken to brethren in Christ, that is, Christians. "Calling," means no less than effectual calling, or regeneration. Election must mean no less than being "chosen unto salvation." Christians, then, are here called upon to make their regeneration and salvation sure. And this is not a command to be regenerated and to receive salvation, for, being Christians, this must have been done already. It must be no less than a command to make it sure, that this *had been done;* in other words, to gain the full assurance of hope. But this command would not have been given, if they could not have been Christians without this assurance.

And in the epistle to the Hebrews, it is said—"And we desire that every one of you do show the same diligence to the full assurance of hope unto the end." Heb. vi. 11. This was spoken, not to sinners, but to those who did "things which accompany salvation," as may be seen from its connexion with the foregoing verses. Here, then, Christians are required to use diligence for the purpose of obtaining full assurance of hope. But this diligence would be perfectly needless, if a man could not be a Christian without assuredly knowing it. All Christians, therefore, do not infallibly *know* that they are Christians. How full is the evidence, then, that the opinion now considered, is an erroneous one.

We have now done with the *falseness* of this sentiment; but we have yet to consider its HURTFUL AND DANGEROUS TENDENCY.

Error in religion is always more or less hurtful, either in preventing good, or in promoting evil.—We are safe only in the truth. It is through the belief of the truth that saints are chosen to salvation. 2 Thess. ii. 13. It is the truth that makes us free from condemnation. John viii. 32. And it is through the truth that we are sanctified. John xvii. 17. The more truth we embrace in our sentiments, the more spiritual good we shall probably secure. In other words, the more error we embrace, the less spiritual good we shall probably secure. All error must be constantly, though perhaps imperceptibly, preventing good and promoting evil; particularly in hindering our growth in grace. But many of the evil effects of the error in question are very perceptible. Some of them let us now consider.

It keeps men from seeking assurance of hope in the only way in which it is to be obtained.—It is to be obtained by a faithful inquiry into the evidences of a saving change of heart, in order to ascertain what those evidences are, and whether those evidences are found in our own hearts and lives. But while men believe that saving faith consists in *believing that Christ is ours*, instead of examining themselves to see whether they have the Christian graces, they will be all the time striving for this supposed 'appropriating faith.' Or, supposing that they have this faith already, they will despise all attention to those graces which afford the only real foundation for the full assurance of hope. Or, should they believe that none can be Christians without certainly knowing it, instead of searching for the only real evidences of a change of heart, they will be idly waiting and longing for some more marvellous change than they have experienced or ought to expect; or for some strange and indescribable manifestation to force them to the irresistible and undoubting persuasion, that they have been born again. Or, wrapping themselves up in the presumptuous belief that they have this irresistible certainty, that they are Christians, they too will despise all attention to the real evidences of a change of heart. Thus it is, that this erroneous opinion keeps those who embrace it from seeking the full assurance of hope in the only way in which it is to be obtained. It is more directly on this account that the error needed to be exposed in this work. It was also necessary, perhaps, to prepare some readers to profit by the two following chapters.

Other evil effects there are, resulting from this erroneous opinion: evil effects which, though they have no direct bearing on the perusal of this work, are still so dangerous that they ought here to be noticed. One is nearly allied to the foregoing.—It is the effect which it has upon religious teachers. If those who are employed to instruct others in "the things of the kingdom," believe that faith consists in believing that Christ died for *us in particular*, and that *we shall assuredly be saved;* or if they believe that the change of heart is of such a nature, that we *cannot* experience it without certainly *know-*

ing it, they will not warn others against self-deception. But how needful such warnings are, we see from the frequency with which they occur in the word of God; and from the many whom we hear expressing assurances of salvation, but who give evidence, nevertheless, that they are strangers to vital godliness. How dangerous it is for religious teachers to withhold these warnings, we see from the need there is of having them administered, and from the confidence which many people put in their spiritual guides. If they hear no warning from them to beware of self-deception, they will conclude their teachers have no doubt of their good estate; and this will lull them into deeper and deadlier confidence respecting their supposed safe estate. Nor is there any calculating what an extensive and fatal influence would result from neglect of these needed warnings.

But this error is especially hurtful, as it leads to *dangerous presumption* on the one hand, and *to needless and distressing despondency* on the other.

It leads to presumption. If any should be persuaded that saving faith consists merely in believing that *Christ died for us in particular;* in other words, that all we have to do, in order to secure our salvation, is to believe *that God intends to save us*, they will be in danger of working themselves up into this presumptuous hope. For all men are constitutionally inclined to believe what they wish to have true. And they who are most insensible of the corruption and deceitfulness of their own hearts, and are most unhumbled in view of their corruption—they who are most impenitent and most self-righteous, will find it most easy to believe without evidence, that they are accepted of God There are many people of a warm, hasty, and rash temperament, that are always ready to adopt what is proposed to them, without much caution or evidence. And others there are, who are so self-conceited and self-importaut, as to believe almost any thing that is in their favour. And if these should drink in the opinion that saving faith consisted in believing *Christ is ours*, how easily could they work themselves up into this presumptuous belief. Such seems to have been the native temperament of the stony-ground hearers spoken of by Christ; and such the event with them. "He that received the seed into stony places, the same is he that heareth the word, and *anon* with *joy* receiveth it; yet *hath he not root* in himself, but dureth for a while: for when tribulation or persecution ariseth because of the word, by and by he is offended." Matt. xiii. 20, 21. In short, the belief that *appropriating faith* is *saving faith*, has a tendency to give those the most confidence of salvation who have the least right to it. And when such a presumptuous hope has gained a place in their hearts, there is a fearful probability that it will lead them down to final wrath. When we consider how eagerly the selfish heart of man clings to a welcome deception; when we consider how much there is in a profession of religion, and in the good opinion in which many self-deceivers stand with mankind, to foster such a delusive hope; and when we consider how seldom such a hope is finally rejected, we cannot but tremble for those who hope they are Christians while they remain the children of wrath. How pernicious, then, is the sentiment that saving faith consists in believing *Christ is ours.*

From the opinion, 'that all who experience a saving change of heart, must assuredly know it,' the like evil effects arise; though not perhaps so directly, or to the same extent. Such as hold to this opinion are very liable to be the dupes of delusion.—Supposing that they must have some marvellous and supernatural manifestation of this change, they will be liable to imagine that what they have expected has arrived. What is looked after and longed for, the interested imagination is very apt to present. And Satan, that arch deceiver, will eagerly seize on the opportunity thus afforded, to present to them the fatal delusion. And thus the supposed appearance of Christ, or of an angel—the recollection of a comforting passage of Scripture—the circumstance that such a passage was the first that met their eye on opening the Bible—the supposition that they have heard a voice pronouncing their sins forgiven—nay, even a pleasant dream, affords them all the grounds they wish, for a full knowledge of their saving change. Or, suppose they look for their evidences in the exercises of the heart. They expect, nevertheless, that these exercises will be so clear, that they cannot mistake in them. This keeps them from suspecting self-deception, and will thereby expose them the more to it. It will keep them from the fear of counterfeit graces, aud thus expose them the more to delusion by them. All those professors of religion, who believe a man cannot be a Christian without knowing it, must, to be consistent, say, that from the time of their regeneration they have absolutely *known* that they were Christians. But if it is not true that 'all Christians must necessarily *know* they are Christians,' we have reason to fear, that many of those who profess to know themselves Christians are deceived. Their deception, then, has most probably grown out of this erroneous opinion.—How pernicious, therefore, must this opinion be.

This error leads, on the other hand, to needless and distressing despondency. While native corruption fosters self-ignorance, self-conceit, pride, and arrogance; grace produces self-acquaintance and humility, and thence self-distrust. And when, by regenerating grace, men are brought to "know every one the plague of his own heart," and to know that this heart is "deceitful above all things;" and when deeply humbled at the sight of it, they are very distrustful of themselves. Nay, many new-born souls are jealous, and suspicious of themselves even to excess. Now, with such a temper of mind, how difficult will it be for them to believe at once and without doubt, that they are the objects of God's approving love and saving grace. And if such are made to believe, that saving faith consists in their believing that God loves *them*, and designs to save them—Christ is theirs, and that therefore they shall assuredly be saved, how will they be distressed, because they cannot have this full and undoubting confidence in the favour of God? With their deep sense of guilt and unworthiness, how difficult will it be for them to exercise this 'appropriating faith;' yet in proportion to their sense of guilt and unworthiness, will be their desire of salvation. How painful, then, will be their persuasion that they cannot exercise the faith by which alone they can be saved?

Equal distress will it give them, to believe that *they cannot be Christians without knowing it.*—They will say within themselves, "I cannot be a Christian, for I do not *know* that what I have experienced is a saving change of heart. I must look for something more wonderful and striking than any thing that I have experienced." This is not uncommon language; especially with those whose conversion is not so clear and striking as that of others. The writer has often heard it; and probably many of his readers have heard it also; and heard it too, from those who manifest, both by conversation and conduct, that they are the regenerated followers of Christ. There are many "who despise the day of small things." They are looking for something great, something that will be so plain an evidence that they can no longer doubt their regeneration: and they do so, because they suppose that they can have *no* evidence, but *certain, irresistible* evidence. And thus they go on in painful despondency for months, perhaps for years.

How much painful despondency is then occasioned by a belief of this erroneous opinion: despondency not only of this but *needless.* Needless, because, if they did not believe that saving faith consisted in a vague, indescribable, yet bold and unhesitating confidence, that they should be saved; nor yet that a change of heart was of such a nature, that none could have it without knowing it; but believed on the contrary, that the question whether they are Christians or not, 'rests on the nature of the exercises of their own hearts;' and that these exercises needed to be examined, and *carefully* examined, before they can know whether they are Christians:—Were *such* their belief, instead of sitting down heartless and hopeless, they would proceed to self-examination; and self-examination, if thorough, would soon lead to a joyful and assured hope that they had passed from death unto life.

I must hope that the reader is now convinced, that the opinion that *saints must of necessity know they are saints, is* FALSE, *is* HURTFUL, *and* DANGEROUS; and that he is therefore guarded against its pernicious effects. I would hope too, that he is prepared for the inquiries, whether the full Assurance of Hope is Attainable? and, How it is to be obtained? To these inquiries let us then proceed.

CHAPTER II.

FULL ASSURANCE OF HOPE SHOWN TO BE ATTAINABLE.

THE question whether it be possible for saints to gain a Full Assurance that they are in a state of salvation, has long been a matter of dispute. It was one point of controversy in the great Reformation. The possibility of attaining to this Assurance, the Papists denied; and the Reformers asserted and supported it. [See Calvin's Institutes, Book iii. Chap. 2.]

In later times too, and even down to the present day, it has been a subject of dispute. The grounds of the controversy, however, are considerably different from that occupied in the Reformation. The Papists resting their expectations of salvation on their own works, denied that Assurance was possible, because it was not possible for a man to know that he should do good works enough to secure salvation. The Reformers, resting their expectations of salvation on the grace of God received by faith in Christ, affirmed that this assurance was possible, because God was unchanging in his designs and promises of grace. But the point now in question is, 'whether we can know that we have secured this unchanging grace of God?' Whether we have that faith on condition, of which God promises salvation? Whether we are those saints whom, in his unchanging purpose, God designs to save?

The possibility of gaining the Full Assurance of Hope, is asserted in the Ecclesiastic Standards of most denominations, who are considered Calvinistic. It makes a part of the "Larger Catechism," adopted by that noted "Assembly of Divines," who met at Westminster, in the year 1643; as will appear from the following quotations.

"Question 80.—Can true believers be infallibly assured that they are in the estate of grace, and that they shall persevere therein unto salvation?

"Answer.—Such as truly believe in Christ, and endeavour to walk in all good conscience before him, may, without extraordinary revelation, by faith grounded upon the truth of God's promises, and by the Spirit enabling them to discern in themselves those graces to which the promises of life are made, and bearing witness with their spirits that they are the children of God, be *infallibly assured*, that they are in the estate of grace, and shall persevere therein unto salvation.

"Quest. 81.—Are all true believers at all times assured of their present being in the estate of grace, and that they shall be saved?

"Ans.—Assurance of grace and salvation not being of the essence of faith, true believers may wait long before they obtain it; and after the enjoyment thereof, may have it weakened and intermitted, through manifold distempers, sins, temptations, and desertions: yet are they never left without such a presence and support of the Spirit of God, as keeps them from sinking into utter despair."

This Catechism is adopted by several Protestant churches, and this doctrine makes, therefore, one article in their several Creeds. Such is especially the case with Congregationalists and Presbyterians on both sides of the Atlantic. Several theologians of these denominations, (Flavel, Baxter, Saurin, Ridgley, Brooks, Edwards, Hervey, Buck, Hopkins, Dwight, and others,) have written in support of this doctrine. THE CONFESSION OF FAITH OF THE PRESBYTERIAN CHURCH, besides including the 'Larger Catechism' alluded to above, has a separate chapter, entitled "OF THE ASSURANCE OF GRACE AND SALVATION," including what is said in the Catechism on the subject, with considerable dilations.

My object in making the foregoing remarks, has been to show the reader that this is no *new doctrine;* lest that prejudice which pronounces every thing to be visionary which appears to be new, should keep him from duly weighing the arguments which I am about to present. And I have been the more particular, because, so far as my observation has extended, those who doubt the doctrine here maintained belong to those denominations whose standards and standard writers I have just mentioned.

But why have these persons so far departed from 'the old land-marks?' It is owing in part, I apprehend, to *ignorance.* Those ecclesiastic standards that assert the possibility of gaining full assurance of hope, and those writings which prove and illustrate it, are not read by Christians in general. And though they often read of it in the word of God, they do not apprehend it. But it is owing more I think to *prejudice,* and a *misguided fear of enthusiastic delusion.* They have often heard professors of another denomination speak contemptuously of a "hope," insisting that 'we must *know* that we are Christians, else we are yet in our sins;' or they have heard many boast that they *knew* they were Christians, while they gave others little evidence of piety; and thus they have been led to think much on the danger of presumption, and the difficulty of obtaining certain evidence of a change of heart. Being thus excessively afraid of presumption, and not discriminating between the opinion that 'the saint *must* know his spiritual state,' and the opinion that 'he *may* know it;' they have gone over to the opposite, and no less erroneous extreme, of supposing that 'he *could not* know his spiritual state.'

Such was once the ignorance and prejudice of the author. Such also was the erroneous opinion to which they led him. And when, by a consultation of the word of God, he was led to the belief that saints could gain the full assurance of hope, he was not aware that this sentiment was to be found in the standards of so great a portion of professing Christians. Nor was it till after he had even progressed considerably in the present work, that he found so many able pens had been employed in support of this sentiment.

Freed from the influence which ignorance and prejudice are wont to exert against this doctrine, let us candidly consider the proofs on which this doctrine rests.

1. *The full assurance of hope is attainable, because it would be derogatory to God's grace to suppose that he would offer us salvation in a way so*

intricate, so difficult to be understood, that we could not possibly know whether we were in possession of it or not. God offers us salvation on condition that we exercise a certain kind of faith in Christ.—This faith we can exercise : and this faith if we *do* exercise, God assuredly will save us. If, then, we cannot be sure of salvation, it is because we cannot know that we have this faith. But does this look like the dealings of a God of infinite condescension and grace? Shall we suppose that he who has provided salvation for us at infinite expense, and who has made such various and vast preparations for putting us in possession of this salvation, should, after all, offer it to us in no other way than one in which we could not possibly know whether we had secured it or not? Shall we suppose that a Being of infinite majesty would trifle thus with his creatures in a concern of such infinite moment?

Besides, faith is not only an *offered privilege*, but a *commanded duty*. God commands us to exercise saving faith. [See John vi. 28, 29. 1 John, iii. 23.] Neglect to exercise this faith, is therefore considered a sin; yea, the heinous sin of making God a liar. 1 John, v. 10. But where is the justice of condemning us for neglecting this duty, if we cannot ascertain whether we neglect or perform it?

The same may be said of all the Christian graces, such as love of complacency to God and to his people, repentance, resignation, humility, and many others. If we knew that we exercised these graces, we should know that we were Christians, consequently that we had the unfailing promise of salvation. If, then, we cannot know that we shall be saved, in other words, if we cannot know that we are Christians, it is because we cannot know that we exercise these Christian graces. Yet we shall be condemned for the want of them. But where, I ask again, is the justice of condemning us for not exercising these graces, when we cannot ascertain whether we exercise them or not?

Do the Scriptures declare the way of salvation so blind, that none who travel in it can know whether they are in it or out of it? No; far from it.—In foretelling the Christian dispensation, said Isaiah, xxxv. 8, "And a highway shall be there, and a way, and it shall be called, The way of holiness; the unclean shall not pass over it, but it shall be for those: *the way-faring men, though fools, shall not err therein.*"

2. *The full assurance of hope is attainable, because holy affections are directly opposite in their nature to sinful ones.* The doctrine of Total Depravity being true, the sinner has *no* holy exercises. If, then, we have *any* holy exercises, we are Christians. And holy exercises are so different, so entirely opposite to sinful ones, that we surely may distinguish between them; consequently we can know whether we have those that are holy or not. What! is it not possible for us to know whether the feelings we exercise towards God are love or hatred? whether we love or hate his service? whether in regard to his commands and dealings we are resigned or rebellious? whether meditation on his character is pleasant or painful? Can we not possibly know whether we hate or love the nature of

sin? whether we hate or love the nature of holiness? whether we like or dislike the Christian on account of his piety? Can we not know whether religion at large, is welcome or unwelcome to us? In a word, are sin and holiness so much alike, that after the utmost scrutiny, we cannot distinguish the one from the other?

It is true there are both genuine and counterfeit affections; and that we are in danger of mistaking the one for the other. It is true the deceitfulness of the heart makes it the more difficult to discriminate between them. But though somewhat *difficult*, it is far from being *impossible*. Still, the one kind of affections is holy, and the other is sinful.—Still, then, they are distinct and opposite in their natures; and therefore they can be discriminated. In other words, we can know which kind of affections we exercise, consequently we can know whether we are Christians or not.

3. *The full assurance of hope is attainable, because it was obtained by saints of old.* Ancient saints gave thanks to God for pardoning mercy. This fact is found on so many pages of divine inspiration, that no individual passages need be quoted in proof of it. But these saints would not have given thanks thus publicly for what they did not feel fully assured that they had received. Ancient saints must then have had this assurance of hope. But we moreover hear from them the very language of assurance.

Said Job, "I *know* that my Redeemer liveth, and that he shall stand at the latter day upon the earth: And though after my skin worms destroy this body, yet in my flesh shall I see God: whom I shall see for myself, and mine eyes shall behold, and not another." Job xix. 25—27.

Said the Psalmist, "As for me, I will behold thy face in righteousness; I shall be satisfied when I awake with thy likeness." Ps. xvii. 15. "Thou shalt guide me with thy counsel, and afterward receive me to glory."—"My flesh and my heart faileth; but God is the strength of my heart, and my portion for ever." Ps. lxxiii. 24, 26.

Said Paul, "I *know* whom I have *believed*, and am persuaded that he is able to keep that which I have committed unto him against that day." 2 Tim. i. 12. "I have fought a good fight, I have finished my course, I have kept the faith: henceforth there is laid up for me a crown of righteousness, which the Lord, the righteous Judge, shall give me at that day." 2 Tim. iv. 7, 8. "I *know* that this shall turn to my salvation."—"To me to live is Christ, and to die is gain."—"I am in a strait betwixt two, having a desire to depart, and to be with Christ, which is far better." Phil. i. 19, 21, 23 See also Rom. viii. 38, 39.

Here, then, is the language of the full assurance of hope. These men having written by divine inspiration, what they record of themselves must be true. These men attained assurance. Assurance is then attainable.

But here it may be said, 'Those ancient saints who made these confident assertions, knew by *divine revelation*, that they were saints. They, then, who are not divinely inspired, cannot know whether they are saints or not.' To this I reply.

In the first place, they that were inspired of old, did not have every thing revealed to them. They had revealed to them those things only which were necessary to advance the cause of religion. And it was no more necessary for the advancement of religion, that this should be revealed to saints *then*, than that it should be revealed to them *now*. Nor is there any intimation in Scripture that it was revealed to men of old, that they should be saved.—Neither does the fact, that they possessed miraculous gifts, afford any certain evidence that they were saints, and therefore would be saved. For many who were not saints were endued with such gifts. The Egyptian magicians wrought miracles, (Ex. vii. 11, 22; and viii. 7.) Balaam prophesied, (Num. xxiv. 1—9.) So did Caiaphas, (John xi. 51.) And yet these men were far from being in the way of salvation.

But in the second place, although these men did know by inspiration that they were subjects of saving grace, we still have sufficient proof to the point. We have proof that other ancients gained the full assurance of hope, and gained it without the aid of direct and personal revelation. The apostles spoke not only of themselves, as having assurance, but of others also; others who were not inspired.

Said Paul to the Corinthian converts, "We know, that if our earthly house of this tabernacle were dissolved, we have a building of God a house not made with hands, eternal in the heavens." 2 Cor. v. 1. Here the apostle is not speaking of himself merely, but also of Corinthian saints, if not Christians in general. "*We* know," that is, himself and other Christians. "We *know*," not we *hope*. We know that *we have* a building, not that a building is prepared for such as happen at last to be found in the faith.

Said John, "We *know* that we have passed from death unto life because we love the brethren." 1 John, iii. 14. Here the apostle is speaking not only of himself, but also of those to whom he wrote. He therefore asserts, that not only he who was inspired, but they who were not inspired, had assurance of having passed from death unto life. To the same amount does he speak in another place.—He says, "We *know that we are of God*, and the whole world lieth in wickedness. And we *know* that the Son of God is come, and hath given us an understanding, that we may know him that is true, and we are in him that is true, even in his Son Jesus Christ." 1 John, v. 19, 20. "And hereby we *know* that we are of the truth, and shall *assure* our hearts before him."—"Hereby we *know* that he abideth in us by the Spirit which he hath given us." 1 John, iii. 19, 24.

Here, then, we have full testimony that not only inspired men, but common Christians, attained in the apostles' days, to the full assurance of hope. But if they could attain to it in the apostles' days, they can attain to it now: for they have no less light now, than was enjoyed in the age of the apostles. Nay, they have all that was then enjoyed, and much more. Besides, the epistles from which we have been quoting, were not intended to be confined in their application and authority to the age in which they were written. They were intended for the use of the church in all succeeding ages. Consequently the passages which we have just been quoting from them, are applicable to the present day. And what is said in these passages of assurance of hope, is said in intimate connexion with certain duties which are as binding now as they were in the apostles' days. If then the apostles spoke *judiciously* in these passages, the full assurance of hope can still be obtained.

4. *The full assurance of hope is attainable, because God commands us to obtain it.* It would be unjust in God to command us to do what we have not power to do. As then he is "a God of truth and without iniquity," as "just and right is he," never does he require us to perform impossibilities. What he commands therefore, we can perform.—If, then he commands us to attain the full assurance of hope, we *can* attain it. And that he does command it, we learn from the following passages of his holy word.

"Examine yourselves, whether ye be in the faith: prove your own selves. Know ye not your own selves how that Jesus Christ is in you, except ye be reprobates?" 2 Cor. xiii. 5. The object of examination is *knowledge*. When, therefore, we are commanded to 'examine ourselves whether we be in the faith,' we are virtually commanded to *know* whether we are in the faith; that is, we are commanded to know whether we are Christians.—But this passage goes farther. "Prove your own selves;" that is, make such a full examination as shall fully discover your spiritual state. But fully to discover our state, is to *know* that state. Hence in the continuation of the same subject it is said.

"*Know* ye not your own selves, how that Jesus Christ is in you, except ye be reprobates?" By considering the general drift of this passage, we shall find it a continuity of repeated, though varied commands, to know whether we are Christians.

"If a man think himself to be something when he is nothing, he deceiveth himself. But let every man prove his own work, and then shall he have rejoicing in himself alone, and not in another." Gal. vi. 3, 4. The meaning of the first clause of this passage is evidently this: 'If a man think himself a Christian when he is not, he deceiveth himself.' And the second clause is an evident caution not to be thus deceived. "But let every man prove his own work." Let him not be deceived—let him not be uncertain; on the contrary, let him 'prove,' let him fully ascertain, whether he is a Christian or not. "Let him *prove his own work;*" that is, let him examine the nature of the supposed work of grace in his heart, to gain sure evidence whether it is *indeed* a work of grace. Or, let him ascertain the true moral character of his daily conduct, to gain full evidence whether he is a Christian or not. For the apostle tells us, "Every one that doeth righteousness is born of God." 1 John, ii. 29. If, then, we prove that our own work is righteousness, is right in *motive* as well as in *form*, we prove ourselves Christians. Here, then, is a command to gain the full assurance of hope.

"And we desire that every one of you do show the same diligence to the *full assurance of hope.*' Heb. vi. 11. As "holy men of God spake as they were moved by the Holy Ghost," this 'desire' was prompted and uttered by inspiration. It is therefore an expression of the will of God. It is, then, his command. He commands us to "give diligence to the full assurance of hope;" that is, to use such a diligence as will result in this assurance. "Wherefore the rather, brethren, give diligence to make your calling and election *sure*." 2 Pet. i. 10. The "calling" here mentioned, cannot mean a 'common call,' or the general invitations of the Gospel; for none need use "diligence," to make it "sure," that he has such a call. It must, therefore, mean what theologians denominate *Effectual calling*, and which is spoken of in Rom. viii. 30; 2 Thess. ii. 14; and 2 Tim. i. 9. It includes no less than that renewing influence of the Spirit by which the sinner is brought to accept salvation.— The command, then, to make our "calling" sure, is no less than a command to make it sure that we have accepted salvation. "Election" is God's "choosing us to eternal life through the sanctification of the Spirit and belief of the truth." 2 Thess. ii. 13. Now, in order to bring this part of the passage to bear on our subject, we do not need to settle the much agitated questions, *when* the elect were chosen, whether "before the foundation of the world," or at the time of their accepting salvation? Neither, *on what account* they were chosen? whether "according to the good pleasure of his will?" or on account of their good works either done or foreseen? For in either case, nothing makes our election *sure to us*, but the assurance that we have been born again. The command to make our calling and election sure, is no less than a command to gain a full assurance of hope. How ample is the proof, then, that the *full assurance of hope is attainable.*

CHAPTER III.

SHOWING HOW THE FULL ASSURANCE OF HOPE IS TO BE OBTAINED.

MANY seem to suppose that hope is entirely involuntary: that whatever degree of it we have, whether a full assurance or the lowest degree of it, it must be produced in us without any resolution or exertion of our own: consequently, that we have no endeavours to make for the purpose of obtaining it; but have only to sit down and quietly wait, till God see fit to give it to us. Very different, however, is the account which the Scriptures give us of it. They tell us *we* have something to do in obtaining it; that we have *much* to do; yea, that we must be "diligent." Their directions are, "Give *diligence* to make your calling and election sure." 2 Pet. i. 10. And "We desire that every one of you do show the same *diligence* to the full assurance of hope unto the end." Heb. vi. 11. Hope, yea, the full assurance of hope, is an exercise of the understanding, and of the understanding alone.—It is the judgment which the mind makes up concerning our own spiritual state: a judgment resting on certain evidences. Consequently it requires the *exertion* of the understanding to search out these evidences, and to make up the judgment upon them.

The Scriptures do indeed tell us that, "The Spirit itself beareth witness with our spirit, that we are the children of God," Rom. viii. 16: that saints are "sealed with the holy Spirit of promise, which is the *earnest* (or pledge) of their inheritance," Eph

i. 13, 14: and that God "hath sealed his saints, and given the *earnest* of the Spirit in their hearts." 2 Cor. i. 22. But these declarations of Scripture do not teach, as some suppose, that hope, or even *assurance* of hope, is produced by the immediate operations of the Spirit, and that therefore there is no need of exertions on the part of saints to obtain or to increase their hope. All the influence of the Spirit on man, is in perfect harmony with his free agency, and in no wise does it supersede the necessity of means. On the contrary, the object of the Spirit's operations is to give *efficacy* to means.—But in the production of *hope* its operations are not so direct as in the production of *love*, *faith*, and other Christian graces. Though the Spirit produces these graces by the use of means, it produces them by a direct agency. But in the production of *hope*, its agency is indirect. It promotes hope by increasing the several Christian graces, thus rendering them more perceptible and plain, so that the understanding can the more easily examine them, and thereby gain the better evidence of a saving change. The Spirit, moreover, fits the mind to examine these graces with the more candour and earnestness. But let the Spirit operate ever so much upon the heart, and produce ever so many evidences of grace, still the understanding must contemplate them and make up its judgment upon them, or no hope is produced. Hope depends ultimately, then, upon the exertion of the understanding.

Thus we see, that the vigorous exertion of the *mental powers* is necessary for attaining the full assurance of hope. We are next to inquire *how* the understanding is to be exerted? As assurance depends on certain evidences, the mind, to attain this assurance, must be exerted in inquiring,

1. What are evidences of a saving change of heart? and

2. Whether we have these evidences?

Thus our subject resolves itself into two parts. We will attend to them in their order.

PART I.

What are evidences of a saving change of heart?

ALL real Christians are heirs of salvation. This truth is so often declared in God's word, and so generally known and believed, that it needs no proof. Whatever proves a man a Christian, proves, then, that he will be saved. Hence that change of heart which makes a man a Christian, we call a *saving* change.

We shall, therefore, use the terms *evidences of a saving change of heart, evidences of Christianity, evidences of grace, and evidences of salvation, &c.* to mean the same thing.

Many things are supposed to be evidences of saving grace, which furnish but doubtful evidence, if any evidence at all. And as many are led astray by these supposed evidences, some of whom we fear are led down to final perdition, and as others are kept long in doubt and distress, who have a right to hope and rejoice in the saving grace of God, it is needful that we consider these doubtful or spurious ones, before we proceed to examine those which are certain and *genuine.*

There is a wonderful proneness in us to take the particular feelings and conduct of supposed Christians, as the only evidences of grace. Many seem to suppose that they must have just the same feelings, and the same *shades*, *extent* and *degree* of feelings, which others speak of having, else they cannot be Christians. Whereas the fact, that these Christians have these affections, is no proof that other Christians have them. Much less is it a proof that all who have them *are* Christians; and all who are destitute of them are *not* Christians. The apostle tells us, that if we ' measure ourselves by ourselves, and compare ourselves among ourselves, we are not wise.' 2 Cor. x. 12. We must not take saints for our standard. We must take the word of God.—In saints there are many evil as well as good things; and we cannot tell which of them are evidences of grace, unless the word of God informs us. To this " sure word of prophecy," and this alone, we must therefore " take heed."

There are several things which are supposed to be evidences while they are not, each of which ought to have a separate attention.

1. *The great distress which a person may endure in conviction, is no evidence of a saving change of heart.* Although this distress produces involuntary outcries, loss of strength, and even swooning, it furnishes no such evidence. " As these emotions may be, and often are, excited by natural as well as Evangelical causes: so when thus excited, they may exist in any supposable degree. The agonies and transports, the agitations of body and of mind, prove, indeed, the *intensity* of the feelings experi-

..ced ; but they do not in the least degree, exhibit either their nature or their cause ; and cannot, therefore, be safely relied on as evidences of religion."*

Nothing is evidence of a change of heart that takes place *before* that change. And as this distress does take place before conversion, it is plainly no evidence. This is quite evident from constant fact. Many who have once been under most agonizing conviction of sin, have been known to go back into stupidity, yea, to fulfil the Scriptures, the returning 'spirit taking to itself seven other spirits more wicked than itself; so that their last state is much worse than the first.'

2. *Sudden and great joy is no evidence.* Let two persons have equal distress in conviction : let one of them be really forgiven and renewed, while the other is deluded into a false hope, and probably both would equally rejoice. Or, rather, the one that is deceived may have the most joy, for the other may be weighed down with such a sense of guilt and unworthiness, as will greatly check his joy : while the other will have nothing of the kind to restrain him. And grace produces self-distrust.— The one that has met with a real change of heart, will therefore be more afraid of self-deception than the other ; and will thereby be more restrained from joy than the other. Great joy is then no evidence of regeneration. It may be the "joy of faith ;" but it may also be the selfish, unsanctified joy of the stony-ground hearers, who " anon *with joy* received the word," but who " had no root" of grace in their hearts. Matt. xiii. 6.

* Dwight.

3. *The fact, that alarming, or comforting passages of Scripture come suddenly and unexpectedly to our minds,* is no evidence. It is supposed by many, that when passages of Scripture are thus suggested to the mind, God must have done it by his immediate and miraculous agency. But if God should awaken the sinner by thus suggesting to him some alarming passage, this would furnish no evidence that conviction thus produced, would be followed by saving conversion. But it is doubtful whether God does bring these passages to the sinner's mind by this immediate agency. However suddenly and powerfully these Scripture declarations may have come to his mind, they probably came in the common course of second causes.—They come to the mind by *recollection;* recollection awakened by the *association of ideas,* just as the greater portion, if not all our recollections, are awakened.

The same may be said of comforting passages.—However mysteriously they may seem to have been suggested, it may be accounted for on philosophic principles. Some assert that in the time of their conviction and supposed conversion, they had such comforting passages of Scripture come to their minds, as they had never before read or heard. In this assertion they are doubtless *not dishonest,* but *mistaken.* They undoubtedly had read or heard these passages, but had entirely forgotten them; and when they come again to the mind, they do not remember any circumstances which attended them, when they previously read or heard them. Hence they appear like *new* ideas, and not like those which had formerly been contemplated. The reason that they do not recollect that they had read or heard these passages, is, when they did formerly read or hear them, they made very little impression on their minds; or it is so long since, that the impression is very much lost.

But it may be asked 'if these passages are so far gone from the memory, how happens it that they are ever recalled?' It is owing to the *new tone of mind.* What accords with our tone of mind we most readily recollect. The musician, for instance, if *sad*, will most readily strike into a *mournful* air; if cheerful, into one more *gay* and *lively*. And this he will often do, without reflecting that he had previously learned the tune which he is now playing: nay, when he recovers from the revery, it may be very difficult for him to call to recollection even the name of the tune on which he has just been employed. Now, the tone of mind which these persons have when such passages occur to the mind, is *new*, is *vivid*, and corresponds more with the nature of these comforting declarations of Holy Writ, than any tone which they ever before felt. No wonder, then, that these long forgotten passages should be called to remembrance. And no wonder that, in such a high state of feeling, when the mind is so much occupied and interested with many important things, they cannot recollect that they had formerly read or heard these passages.

But if such portions of Scripture never had been read or heard by them, and if therefore they must have come to their minds through some super-human agency, it does not necessarily follow, that

God suggested them by direct miraculous power. They may have been suggested by Satan, "transforming himself into an angel of light." 2 Cor. xi. 14. We should therefore "believe not every spirit, but try the spirits whether they are of God." 1 John, iv. 1.

4. *The fact that the Saviour or an angel of ligh has appeared to us, or an audible voice seems to have spoken to us pronouncing our sins forgiven*, is no evidence. In all this also may Satan have transformed himself into an angel of light to deceive us. But there is no need of attributing these things to satanic influence. They may all be accounted for on natural principles. All these appearances are probably nothing more than what, in the philosophy of mind, is called *Ideal Presence.* When we are so occupied in thought about absent objects, as to give them the exclusive attention of the mind, those objects appear to be really present. This appearance of the absent objects is called *ideal*, in distinction from *real* presence; and always takes place when we imagine that we see some strange sights. It ever occurs when we think we see some super-human beings. These beings are not really present, but we are so full of the thought of them, that they *appear* to be present. No wonder, then, when persons are deeply concerned about their salvation, and are poring over it with undivided attention, Christ or angels should seem to be present; for the One is the Author of salvation, and the others are his messengers of mercy. If, then, these beings should thus appear to us, the fact would be no proof that we had passed from death

unto life. This appearance might happen to the sinner as well as to the saint.

And if these beings may in this way appear to our *sight*, they may in the same way appear to our *hearing*. On the same principle of *ideal presence*, Christ or an angel may seem to speak with an audible voice, pronouncing our sins forgiven, while all is mere imagination. Neither then does this furnish any proof of a saving change of heart.

5. *The fact that we have had remarkable dreams and apparent visions*, is no evidence. For aught we know, all this also may be effected through the influence of Satan transforming himself into an angel of light. If permitted, he would as readily suggest thoughts to deceive us when asleep as when awake. Here too, we should 'try the spirits whether they are of God.' God used once to speak to man in dreams; and I will not say that in some rare instances he does not speak thus to them still. Yet, how are we to know whether our dreams come from God or from Satan?

But those remarkable dreams which are related with so much wonder, which are so confidently rested upon as of divine production, and therefore as furnishing full evidence of a saving change, may all be fairly accounted for on the natural principles which commonly prevail in dreaming. Metaphysicians tell us that our dreams are influenced by our habits, our employments, and our prevailing temper of mind. But we need not go to the learned for this information. We can learn it from daily experience and observation. For how common is it for us to dream about those things which make up our daily employment? especially if we are deeply concerned about them. How common is it for our dreams to vary according to the temper or tone of our minds? If in a happy frame of mind when awake, the dreams in succeeding sleep will generally be pleasant. If the previous tone be sorrowful, the succeeding dreams will be unpleasant. If exposed to danger on the previous day, we shall be subject to alarms in the dreams of the night.—No wonder, then, that after we have been in deep distress for fear of damnation, and our minds exerted to their utmost tension in seeking salvation, no wonder that we have some strange dreams in relation to spiritual things. And God *can* renew our hearts, and awaken in us all the holy affections of the new man, while we are asleep. Yea, I for one, am constrained to believe, that he sometimes actually does so. And whether the new heart be given *in* sleep or immediately *preceding* it, no wonder that in our dreams, our thoughts and feelings should be of altogether a different nature from what we ever had before. Pleasant dreams, then, *may* be the result of regeneration. But they may also result from other things. The self-deceived, who think they are born again, while they are not, may have equal joy when awake; and this may lead to dreams equally strange and delightful with those which are had by the really regenerate. Nay, such dreams may be had by such as have no previous hope that they have been born again. Great distress of mind may lead them to *dream* of great distress, such as exposure on a dangerous precipice, and falling from it; or confinement in a dark or fiery prison. And nothing would be more natural after dreaming of these things, than to dream also of deliverance from them. Indeed, I believe that most generally when we dream of *exposure*, we dream also of *deliverance*. How rash and dangerous would it be, then, to take a *dream* of deliver ance for sufficient *evidence* of deliverance from the wrath to come? Dreams then are no evidence either for or against the security of our salvation.

6. *Zeal in the cause of religion* is no evidence. Every one must have some 'zeal of God,' or he cannot be a Christian. But all zeal in good things is not *Christian* zeal. The Jews had a "zeal of God," but it was "not according to knowledge." Rom. x. 2. We may think we "contend earnestly *for* the faith," while we are only contending *about* the faith, contending only for *mastery*. We may think ourselves "zealous of good works," when we are only zealous for a party. We may contend ever so earnestly for orthodoxy, and yet have no right motives in doing so. And zeal is not characterized by the *subject* on which it is employed, but by the *motives* by which it is prompted.—We may be actuated by the sheerest selfishness in our most earnest endeavours to build up the interests of religion. Neither is zeal characterized by its *intensity*, or degree. We may have all the zeal of a Jehu, and yet be as destitute of piety as he.—Yea, we may have such zeal as would lead us to "give our body to be burned," and yet be destitute of that "charity" or love, without which our zeal will 'profit us nothing.' 1 Cor. xiii. 3.

7. *Great exactness in the external duties of religion*, is, in itself, no evidence. We may have all "the form of godliness," and not have "the power" of it. How exact were the Scribes aud Pharisees: yet Christ said, "Except your righteousness shall exceed the righteousness of the Scribes and Pharisees, ye shall in no case enter into the kingdom of heaven." Matt. v. 20. Many modern formalists are very strict in the outward duties of religion, who, nevertheless, are living very profligate lives. And if the strictness of Scribes, Pharisees, and formalists, in their outward duties, is no evidence of their having saving grace, then our strictness in the same things is no evidence that *we* have saving grace. We may be led to such exactness by education and habit, by example, and by a desire to conform to those around us. We may be led to it because we think such attention to externals will procure us salvation, and therefore we dare not neglect them. Or like the Scribes and Pharisees, we may do it for the sake of being distinguished among our fellow men for our superior piety. Among all these, there may be no holy motives. And as motives give actions their moral character, in that strictness to which these motives prompt, there is no real piety. Ever so great strictness in the externals of religion is no proof then of internal piety.

8. *Great exactness in the discharge of moral duties*, is no evidence. It is true that where religion does exist, it will promote morality. But persons may be outwardly and strictly moral without religion. There are various selfish and sinful motives which may, nay, which often do influence men to

moral duties. They may therefore attend to these duties without any saving grace in their hearts.—Many are very strict in their outward observance of the second table of the law, who neglect the first table altogether. Nay, the Deist who makes a mock of Christianity, is often very strict in moral duties: and is the more so, because morality is all the religion which he believes in; and therefore he wishes to display it as much as he can, that he may gain adherents and applause.

But this point is settled by divine inspiration.—We are informed (Mark x.)that the young man who came to Christ, inquiring what good thing he must do to have eternal life, had observed the several duties of morality. Yet Christ told him, "one thing thou lackest." That 'one thing' was saving grace. Outward morality is then no evidence of salvation.

9. *The fact that we know the exact time when our supposed conversion took place,* is no evidence. We often hear people speak of the precise moment when God pardoned their sins and renewed their hearts. And they evidently speak of knowing the exact time as if it were a matter of great importance; nay, as if it were the highest evidence of the reality of their conversion. We know the exact time when we experienced certain new and strange sensations! What does this prove? It proves this, and this only—that we know the exact time when we were either *converted* or *deceived:* it proves that we had some new religious feelings, either *genuine* or *spurious.* But *which* of the alternatives it does not decide. This is self-evident, and needs no further argument.

As the before mentioned things are not evidences that we are Christians; so on the other hand, the *want* of them is no evidence that we are *not* Christians.

The fact that we have not had very distressing conviction of sin, is no evidence that we are not born again. In the antecedents of conversion, "there are diversities of operations, but the same Spirit." There is every variety both in the mode and degree of convictions. There is no calculating how deep a sense of sin, or how great a fear of wrath, we must have in order to be born again.—Many of the most faithful saints have had but comparatively slight distress for fear of final wrath. It is no uncommon thing for the new-born soul for a long time to reject a hope of salvation, because 'he has not yet been sufficiently convicted.' It is important, therefore, to consider, that while on the one hand we may have ever so distressing conviction, and yet go back into stupidity: on the other hand, though we have ever so little fear of punishment, we may repent and believe; and if we do repent and believe, we are subjects of a saving change of heart.

That we have never had very great and sudden joy, and very wonderful manifestations in divine things, is no evidence against us. As there are various operations of the Spirit *before* conversion, so there are equally various ones *after* it. No two can be found who had exercises in conversion alike, either in degree or circumstances. If we consult the experience of real Christians, we shall find that but a small portion of them had very sudden and high rapture at the time of conversion.—There are many faithful and devout saints who have never known any thing about those sudden transports of which some speak. Shall we on this account refuse them a place among the righteous?—

The Scriptures no where speak of this sudden and great joy as the necessary attendant of a change of heart. Nor when they give us account of certain conversions, do they say any thing of this wonderful joy. By what authority, then, do we declare either that we or others cannot be Christians without it?

The same may be said of the *sudden suggestion of alarming or comforting passages of Scripture*, of *voices*, of *the appearance of super-human beings*, and of *remarkable dreams* and *visions*. They are what very few Christians have ever had. Why then should *we* expect them? Especially, why should we think we cannot be Christians without them? The Scriptures do not tell us that these precede conversion; nor do they tell us of a single instance of conversion, (the apostle Paul's excepted,) in which any of these things happened.

The want of great zeal and exactness in religion, and of great strictness in moral duties, is no *conclusive* evidence that we are not Christians. It is, indeed, the duty of Christians to be very zealous in religion, and to be very punctual in religious and moral duties. But they are none of them as zealous and exact as they ought to be. And who can tell how much they may be wanting in these respects, and yet be Christians? They may not have their attention directed to these things immediately after conversion, being at first completely occupied with other things. And after they have once been zealous and faithful, they may grow very cold and negligent. This coldness and negligence do, indeed, *darken* evidence, but they do not *destroy* it. Some attention there must be to outward duty to God and man, or there is no religion. But to how great an amount, the Scriptures do not inform us. The fact then that we have not a certain *degree* of zeal in religion, or of strictness in religious and moral duties, furnishes no certain evidence that we are not Christians.

And the fact that we know not the exact time when our change of heart took place, is no evidence that it has not taken place. Inquire into the experience of the most faithful Christians, and you will find many of them can form no judgment of the precise time when they passed from death unto life. The change, though great and instantaneous, is with many so imperceptible as not at once to be apprehended. It needs some time to unfold itself. And to some, it unfolds itself so gradually, that they are unable to ascertain the very point when the change took place. But if the change *has* taken place, what matters it if we cannot tell *when* it took place? And if we have sufficient evidence that we *have* experienced a real saving change of heart, why should we doubt it, because we do not know its date? If we saw the sun actually *risen*, what folly to doubt its being up because we did not see it at the *moment of its rising*. And when we have evidence that we have saving grace in exercise, it is equally foolish to doubt it, because we do not know when its exercise began. Yet how many are needlessly distressing themselves with the fear that they have never been born again, because they know not the exact time when their change took place.

In our inquiry, then, 'whether we are Christians?' we are to lay the things above named entirely out of the account. We are to have no regard at all to the degree of distress which we had in conviction, nor the degree of joy which we had in conversion. We are not to consider whether God has mysteriously suggested certain portions of his word to our minds; whether we have heard a voice from some invisible being; seen any strange sights; or had any remarkable dreams. Nor are we to measure the intensity of our zeal, or the extent of our punctuality in the outward duties of religion and morality. But we are to proceed in our inquiries just as if these things had nothing to do with our conversion and salvation.

Having now considered those things which many suppose to be evidences of grace, but which are *not* evidences, we come next to consider what *are* evidences. And as regeneration is the entrance into a state of salvation, it may be expected that I describe that change, with its attendant symptoms.—But the object of this treatise, is not so much to aid the *young convert* in the attainment of a *hope*, as to aid *all saints* to attain *full assurance* of hope. And as with many who are destitute of this assurance, the day of their conversion has long since gone past, they have forgotten many of the symptoms which attended it. A description of regeneration, with its common attendants, would do them little good.—

Nay, it would do the young convert but little good. For in the first place, the attendant symptoms of regeneration are very various. No two cases can be found which are very much alike; and many cases are widely different. And where so vast a variety obtains, it would be difficult to point out all those different combinations which happen in so many different cases. And it would be still more difficult for the young convert to find a combination to suit his own case so nearly as to furnish sufficient evidence that he has passed from death unto life.

In the next place, much of that high and ardent feeling which is generally experienced immediately after conversion, is mere animal fervor. With those holy affections which grace has awakened in the new-born soul, there is mingled many a high emotion which nothing but novelty excited. The sudden transition from a prospect of endless misery to that of eternal blessedness, awakens the highest degree of joyful wonder and surprise. Many new emotions which are supposed to be prompted by grace, are excited by nothing but the new condition in which the soul is now placed.

It is very generally supposed, that the day of our conversion is the best time to examine the grounds of our hope. And I believe many with whom that day is long past, attempt to call it to remembrance, as if they thought a recollection of what they then felt, was the best way of examining their hope.—But this is far from being true. The best time to examine our spiritual state, is when those emotions which adventitious circumstances had awakened, have somewhat subsided, and when little is left of a gracious appearance but what grace itself has excited.* It is true that at such a time we have not that assistance of *contrast*, which we had near the time of conversion; but this is more than overbalanced by the circumstances just named.

For these reasons, I shall confine myself to those evidences of grace which obtain with the Christian in every stage of his spiritual life. These evidences are none other than the holy exercises of the new heart. Of these I shall consider those only which are the most essential, and the most easily understood. They are LOVE, RESIGNATION, HUMILITY, HATRED OF SIN, and DELIGHT IN HOLINESS.

I. LOVE.—As this grace has its several branches, each of which forms a separate and sufficient proof of regeneration, as it is the fountain from which many, if not all the other graces flow, as so many different streams; and as it is a grace concerning which we are most liable to be deceived, we shall need to examine it at considerable length.

The apostle tells us "Love is of God, and every one that *loveth* is *born of God*, and knoweth God." 1 John, iv. 7. Love, then, is evidence of conversion, and therefore of salvation. But all men exercise the passion of love, yet all are not Christians. The love here spoken of, must then be of a particular moral quality. It must be a *holy* love in dis-

* NOTE.—The young convert, however, should not delay his self-examination, till the effects of novelty subside; for he is bound to know his state immediately: and before these effects of novelty subside, death may overtake him.

tinction from natural love. Its nature therefore demands our special attention. And to ascertain its nature, we must consider separately its *kinds* and its *objects*.

Its kinds are three, viz.: *Love of benevolence, love of complacency*, and *love of gratitude.*

Love of benevolence, is good will. It is a desire for the welfare of its object; a desire which prompts to acts of kindness, where such kindness can be exercised.

Love of complacency, is a delight in, and an approbation of, moral conduct and character. It is love of moral excellence. Or, rather, it is attachment to a being because he possesses such excellence.

Love of gratitude, is the affection which we feel towards a being for the kindness or good will which he has shown to us. Gratitude is not gladness at the receiving of a benefit, as many suppose. It is felt not toward the *gift*, but toward the *giver*. It is regard for the benevolence of the benefactor, not for the benefit which we derive from the benefaction. And where the person perceives that the kindness was not shown from benevolent, but from selfish, sinful ends, though he may have joy in the benefit, yet strictly speaking, he can have no gratitude. So on the other hand, if we see a man truly desirous to do us a favour, but is not able, we may feel a real gratitude for his good will, while we receive no benefit from it. Gratitude is, then, altogether another thing from gladness on account of a favour received.

The objects of holy love are three, viz.: GOD, *saints*, and *sinners.*

To God all these three kinds of love are exercised. To the notion that saints exercise the love of benevolence to God, some have objected. They say, this cannot be, because God cannot be profited by his creatures. But can we not desire to have that done which we cannot aid in accomplishing? Can we not show our good wishes where we cannot put forth any profiting exertions? Surely we can. But this is benevolence. And are not the glory of God, and the good of his kingdom, desirable? If the finite happiness of man is desirable, is not the happiness, that is, the *blessedness* of God, vastly more desirable? We exercise benevolence to God, then, in *good wishes.* And can we not in *good works* also? Said Christ, "Herein is my Father glorified, that ye bear much fruit." John xv. 8. Can we not then strive to live holy, that we may thereby glorify God?

The love of good will is, then, exercised toward God. And this branch of love is one of the most striking evidences of a change of heart. For the unrenewed sinner has no desire to have God's will done, to have his glory advanced, or the good of his kingdom promoted. The tenor of his feelings and conduct is in direct opposition to these things. He opposes God's will, is constantly and earnestly engaged in the work of mischief to the cause of religion; and if left to himself with sufficient power, he would rob God of his glory and tear him from his throne. And when completely turned about in all these respects, how manifest the evidence of a saving change.

6 *

But this branch of love has its *counterfeits.* It is important, therefore, that there should be some test by which it may be tried. And such a test I think we have. True love of benevolence toward God, will lead a man to obedience, for the purpose of pleasing God, of advancing his kingdom and glory. To try our love, we must therefore inquire whether it *leads* us to corresponding endeavours to obey God. I say not is *attended* with these endeavours, for attendant obedience may be prompted by selfish, sinful motives, in which case it affords no evidence that our love is genuine. It is only when our love to God *leads* us to desire and thus to endeavour to serve God, that we have any reason to think that we have genuine love of benevolence toward God.

The love of *complacency* is confessedly exercised towards God. And it undoubtedly is this kind of love which the Scriptures generally intend, where they promise salvation to those who love God.—"God keepeth covenant and mercy for them that love him." Neh. i. 5. "Delight thyself in the Lord, and he shall give thee the desire of thine heart." Ps. xxxvii. 4. "The Lord preserveth all them that love him." Ps. cxlv. 20. "All things work together for good to them that love God." Rom. viii. 28. "Eye hath not seen, nor ear heard, neither have entered into the heart of man, the things which God has prepared for them that love him."1 Cor. ii. 9. "Heirs of the kingdom which he hath promised them that love him." James ii. 5. Here, then, is full testimony that love of complacency toward God, is evidence of salvation.

But many are apt to think that they have this love, while they have it not; and thus they are exposed to fatal delusion. Its nature needs, therefore, to be particularly pointed out.

Love of complacency to God, is a love to his whole moral character. This character is made up of his several moral attributes or perfections. If then, we leave part of these attributes out of the consideration, we do not consider his whole character. So to exercise a love of complacency to only a part of his perfections, is not to approve of his whole moral character—is not to approve of his *real* character. And here it is, that persons are most apt to be deceived. They love only his attributes of benevolence grace, compassion, and forbearance. But as these are not all the essential attributes that make up his character, in loving these only, they do not love the true God, but a figment of their own formation. The true God is not only forbearing, compassionate, good and gracious; but he is holy, righteous, and sovereign.—To have that love of complacency to him which is evidence of regeneration, we must approve of his *holiness;* that is, of his freedom from sin, and his abhorrence of it—we must approve of his *righteousness* or *justice*, as displayed in the condemnation and eternal punishment of the finally impenitent—we must approve of his *sovereignty* as exercised in "working all things after the counsel of his own will," and overruling all things for the advancement of his own glory. If we love those attributes only which we apprehend to be exercised in doing *us good;* we love him merely because he *loves us.*—

And says Christ, "If ye love them which love you, what thank have ye? for *sinners also love those that love them.*" Luke vi. 32. Here, then, it is important to discriminate.

The love of *gratitude* is exercised toward God. This is looked upon by some with no little suspicion. They consider it to be a *selfish* affection, and are therefore reluctant to admit it as a *holy* one. But this arises from their misapprehension of its nature; apprehending it to be a *joy* in the *benefit* received, while it is no other than *esteem* for the *giver*, esteem for the good will which prompted to the kindness experienced. It is, however, to be feared that many do not distinguish between them, and thus are dangerously deceived. But if we do plainly discern that what we feel is real gratitude to God, we gain thereby a real evidence of a saving change of heart: for this is an affection of which the unrenewed sinner is represented in Scripture to be destitute. [See Luke vi. 35; Rom. i. 21; 2 Tim. iii. 2.] But the saint is frequently said to exercise it. Said John, "We love God, because he first loved us." 1 John, iv. 19. And the Revelator tells us that the final song of the redeemed will be, "Thou art worthy—for thou wast slain, and hast redeemed us to God by thy blood." Rev. v. 9. Here, then, gratitude is declared by inspiration to be the appropriate exercise of saints on earth and in heaven. And is not the saving grace of God which we have experienced, worthy of our gratitude? Should we not act a very unchristian part if we did not exercise it? On the other hand, if we do exercise this affection, do we not discharge an important Christian duty? Must we not therefore be Christians?

Still, however, this kind of evidence is to be rested on with great caution. For there is vast danger of mistaking a selfish gladness at the gift, for gratitude to the Giver. Probably, too, there is an emotion somewhat similar to gratitude: an emotion which arises *naturally, instinctively, involuntarily* in the heart, on the reception of a favour: an emotion which being involuntary, has no moral character: an emotion which, however, is liable to contribute to much moral evil; because it is that kind of feeling on which all indirect bribery is founded. It is important, then, not only that we distinguish between gladness and gratitude, but that we discern whether the emotion which we call gratitude, is voluntary or *involuntary:* whether we are led to the exercise of this affection by a sense of duty; whether we lament that we have so little, and strive to have more of it: or whether our affection is a mere animal and instinctive feeling, unattended with any sense of obligation? And a faithful inquiry of this kind will save us from fatal error.

Toward CHRISTIANS are these three kinds of love exercised. Love to the saints is what is so often spoken of in Scripture under the denomination of 'brotherly love,' or 'love of the brethren.' It affords the highest proof of a change of heart.—"We *know* that we have passed from death unto life, because we love the brethren." 1 John, iii. 14. And said Christ, "By this shall *all men know* that ye are my disciples, if ye have love one to another." John xiii. 35. Love to the brethren can be more easily examined and understood, than love to God. The being of God is so incomprehensible, and his attributes so various, and so difficult to be understood, that it is not so easy a task to ascertain whether we do actually love him. But the character of Christians is more easily comprehended. It is, therefore, less difficult to examine the nature of our love to them. But even this is not without its difficulties and dangers. Here also we need caution.

Love of *benevolence* is most especially to be exercised toward Christians. Said David, "My goodness extendeth not to thee, but to the saints that are in the earth." Ps. xvi. 2, 3. And says the apostle, "As we have therefore opportunity, let us do good unto all men, especially unto them who are of the household of faith." Gal. vi. 10. And this individual branch of love to Christians, is full evidence of grace. For the sinner never has this love to the saint. Said Christ to his followers, "But because ye are not of the world, but I have chosen you out of the world, therefore the world hateth you." John xv. 19. That sinners have a deep rooted dislike to saints, is proven also by universal observation and experience. And it is evident that the sinner feels no kindness toward an object that he hates. It is not, however, contended that the sinner does the saint no kind *acts;* but that these acts are not the offspring of any kind *feelings*, at least any *benevolent* feelings. The motives that move him to this kindness are some way selfish.—Here then is the difficulty. It is to ascertain the motive which prompts us to kind acts toward the saints. If we know that they are the offspring of real *good will* to them, we may rest assured that "we have passed from death unto life."

Love of *complacency* toward Christians, demands more attention. It is perhaps the most important test of regeneration. Its nature, therefore, should be more thoroughly examined. Many mistake this love for a certain respect and reverence for the Christian. But this affection of theirs keeps them at a distance from the Christian, while a real love of complacency would draw them nigh to him. It is attended with no desire to be like him, while real love of complacency is a delight in the holy affections and holy duties which make up the Christian character; and is therefore attended with a desire to possess those things, and thus to follow him as he follows Christ.

Many again may suppose they love the Christian, because the saints with whom they associate, are possessed of interesting intellectual endowments, or of an amiable temper, or engaging manners, or some other charms which *nature* confers. But all these a person may have, and not be a Christian. Love to a person for these natural endowments, is not then the love of grace, but the love of *nature's most amiable and interesting forms.* Whereas the real love of complacency toward Christians, is a love to *Christian character.* It is a love of God's own image as seen in the face of his children. It is a love to this image, wherever it is found, whether in the ignorant or the learned, in the rich or the poor, in the comely or the deformed. And the way to test it, is to inquire whether we love the Christian truly for his *piety:* and whether we should still love him, although we saw him never so much degraded in his temporal estate.

The love of *gratitude*, as exercised toward *saints*, is not a very distinguishing evidence of regeneration; and will therefore need no particular attention.

Toward SINNERS, only two kinds of holy love can be exercised: the love of *benevolence*, and the love of gratitude. There is nothing in the moral character of the sinner which ought to meet with the love of complacency. "Every imagination of the thoughts of his heart is *only* evil *continually*." Gen. vi. 5. To exercise love of complacency toward such a character, would be very wicked; and would be a strong proof that we were *not* Christians. The language of true piety in relation to the character of the wicked, is, "Do not I hate them, O Lord, that hate thee? I hate them with perfect hatred." Ps. cxxxix. 21, 22. But while we dislike his conduct, we should earnestly desire the sinner's welfare.

The love of *benevolence* is then exercised by the saint toward the sinner. It is but that love to our neighbours which is commanded in the moral law; and which includes all the duties which we owe to our neighbours. Matt. xxii. 37—40. Rom. xiii. 10.

This love is an evidence of salvation, for none but the saint ever exercises it. The sinner may suppose that he exercises it, because he does the *acts* of kindness. But his acts of kindness are prompted by other feelings than those of good will. They are prompted by the motives of mere selfishness. He never desires the prosperity of his fellow men, in itself considered. But just so soon as grace enters the heart, this love is begun.

Yet this love becomes a prominent evidence of grace only when it extends to all mankind, and when exercised in relation to their salvation. The sinner thinks only of those who are within his own circle or neighbourhood; at most, of those in his own country. And because interest has led him to anxiety or exertion for their good, in order the better to secure his own, he thinks he exercises toward them the love of benevolence. But the moment this sinner becomes a saint, he sends his views abroad to the whole human family. He feels for them *all*, even for his enemies, a disinterested good will, which he felt before for *none*. And all the sinner's anxiety about his fellow sinners, is for their temporal good. But just so soon as he becomes a saint, he awakes to a deep concern for the mighty interest of their souls. He longs for their salvation. This love is therefore an evidence of a saving change of heart. Especially is it so, when it is exercised in not only *forgiving enemies*, but in earnestly supplicating their salvation and forgiveness from God.

Love of *gratitude* may be exercised toward sinners. But as it has no characteristic which makes it a prominent evidence of a new heart, it demands no separate attention here.

II. Resignation.—This is the submitting of *our* will to the will of *God*. It is what was expressed by Christ when he said to his Father, "Not as *I* will, but as *thou* wilt." Matt. xxvi. 39. It consists not in listless indifference respecting God's dealings with us. Christ uttered the foregoing expression of submission in relation to his approaching sufferings on the cross: sufferings, the prospect of which was then filling him with appalling agony. Nor is resignation a willingness to sūbmit to those of God's dealings which are in themselves desirable. In such dealings, there is no room for the exercise of this grace.

Resignation has respect both to the present and the future. In relation *to present*, it is often called *submission*, and is what the apostle enjoins when he says, "Submit yourselves therefore to God." James iv. 7. In relation *to future*, it is *confidence*, and is what is so often enjoined in Scripture under the denomination of trust in God. Resignation is the surrender of ourselves, both body and soul to God, to have him order all our destiny both for the present and the future, both for time and eternity. It is a willingness to have him command of us what services he pleases, to lay upon us what sufferings in life he pleases, and appoint us what final destiny he pleases.

Resignation is not a *necessary* or *constrained* submission. It is not a yielding to the will of God because we cannot resist it. But it is a deliberate choice to have God order our interest, rather than to order it ourselves: a choice produced by the consideration that God *knows* what is best; will *choose* what is best, and is able to *do* what is best: what is best, if not for *us*, at least for the *general good*. It is a confidence in the wisdom, goodness, and power of God. It is an *entire* surrender. It makes no secret reservations, but gives up all. It is a *cheerful* surrender. It is attended with a degree of satisfaction at the thought of being entirely at God's disposal.

Resignation furnishes one of the clearest evidences of a new heart. The unrenewed sinner is not *resigned* but *rebellious.* The apostle tells us, "The carnal mind is enmity against God; for it is not subject to the law of God, neither indeed can be." Rom. viii. 7. None will cheerfully submit to the direction and disposal of one to whom they have no love, and in whom they have no confidence. Especially will they not submit thus to one against whom they feel a positive enmity. Yet such an enmity the sinner has toward God. While, then, he has this enmity of *the carnal* mind toward God, he will exercise none of that *deliberate, entire* and cheerful submission which has here been described. The moment, then, that he does exercise it, his heart of enmity is gone—he has a new heart—he is a Christian.

Resignation is the highest testimony of our approbation of God's will; as it requires us to give up our own will, and to deny ourselves those things which appear to be for our own welfare.

Resignation *is evidence* of a saving change of heart, because it is one ingredient in *saving faith.* I mean a reliance on the moral excellence of God's character. He then that is resigned to God's sovereign will, must evidently exercise a saving reliance on his grace. And many are the promises which are made to those who have such confidence in God. "The Lord redeemeth the soul of his servants: and none of them that *trust* in him shall be desolate." Ps. xxxiv. 22. "Blessed is the man that maketh the Lord his trust." Ps. xl. 4. See also Ps. cxxv. 1; Prov. xvi. 20; Isaiah xxvi. 3; Jeremiah xvii. 7.

III. HUMILITY.—This is lowliness of mind.—It consists in a willingness to take our proper place, the place that belongs to us. It is an apprehension that we are nothing in comparison with God; and that we have nothing to boast of in comparison with our fellow men. It is a sense of our frailty, our inability, of our entire dependence upon God for every good thing. Especially is it a deep sense of our unworthiness on account of our sins. It is the opposite of pride, arrogance, and ambition. Humility manifests itself in patience under sufferings, because they are no more than we deserve; and in meekness, forbearance and forgiveness under injuries, because we have sinned, and our offended Saviour has forborne with us, has forgiven us, and commands us to follow his example. It manifests itself in a proper modesty before our superiors, a moderation before our equals, and a condescension to inferiors. It manifests itself in an unaspiring contentment in the place which God allots to us, and a readiness to ascribe all the good we enjoy to the unmerited goodness of God.

Such humility must be proof of a change of heart; for the natural heart is proud and self-dependent. Hence infidels have arrayed themselves against this virtue, declaring it to be the extremity of meanness. This grace, then, is not of nature's growth. Wherever it is found, therefore, it *must have been implanted* by the saving grace of God.

Moreover, the Scriptures virtually declare that humility is an evidence of grace. "For thus saith the high and lofty One that inhabiteth eternity, whose name is Holy, I dwell in the high and holy place, with him also that is of a contrite and *humble* spirit, to revive the spirit of the *humble*, and to revive the heart of the contrite ones." Isaiah lvii. 15. The Scriptures assure us that "God shall save the *humble* person." Job xxii. 29. That "he resisteth the proud, and giveth grace to the *humble*," (1 Pet. v. 5.)—that "he that shall *humble* himself, shall be exalted," (Matt. xxiii. 12.)—that "whosoever shall *humble* himself as this little child, the same is greatest in the kingdom of heaven." Matt. xviii. 4. But none are heirs to these beatitudes but the children of God. Humility, then, is an evidence of saving conversion.

But if we would not deceive ourselves, we must consider that humility is not an external appearance, but an internal grace. It consists not in the shape of a bonnet, the cut of a coat, or the colour and quality of our clothing. It is true that humility will make us more indifferent about the appearance of our dress. But on the other hand, a very plain dress may cover a very proud heart.

Humility does not consist in thinking ourselves worse than we are. This is merely an error in judgment. Neither does it consist in *thinking worse* of ourselves than of others. It is true that a man under a deep sense of his vileness and guilt, will see more of himself than of others, and will therefore be led to think himself worse than others. But in this case, his humility is to be measured by his view, not of his *relative*, but of his *positive* abasement. Much less does humility consist *in declaring* ourselves to be worse than others. It is true that many are influenced by humility to make this declaration, and to make it honestly, when they are thought to be insincere. But it may be made out of mere hypocrisy. Least of all does humility consist in speaking of ourselves in terms of reproach and contempt. Deep humility will prompt us, it is true, to the language of self-loathing. But this same language may be used out of mere affectation; nay, out of a most pitiful desire to call forth the praise of others. It is the humility of the *heart* only that evinces a *new* heart.

IV. Hatred of Sin.—By this, I mean a dislike to sin on account of its ugly and odious nature, and of its deforming and defiling effects. It is a dislike to sin wherever it is seen, whether in others or ourselves. It is a dislike to sinful feelings and desires, as well as to sinful conversation and conduct. It is a hatred to it not merely for its mischievous effects, but for its intrinsic odiousness. It will lead to sorrow for the past, and to reformation for the future.

That this affection is full testimony of a saving change of heart, is evident from the fact, that the unregenerate love sin. The sinner "drinketh in iniquity like water." Job xv. 16. "Wickedness is sweet in his mouth, he hides it under his tongue, he spares it and forsakes it not, but keeps it still within his mouth." Job xx. 12, 13. If this heart which naturally loves sin, now hates it, this heart must have been changed by the saving grace of God.

Beside, this hatred of sin is the very foundation of all evangelical repentance. This repentance is a sorrow for the sins that we have heretofore committed, because those sins are *hateful.* The reason that the unregenerate do not repent of sin, is, they *love* it. The reason that the regenerate do repent of sin, is, they *hate* it. In other words, hatred to sin leads to repentance. This hatred of sin, then, must be full evidence of a change of heart. Every passage of Holy Writ which promises salvation to repentance, promises it by consequence to hatred of sin.

But there is danger of thinking we have this Christian grace, while we are utter strangers to it. Hatred to sin is often mistaken for *dread of its punishment.* Yet the one is altogether different from the other. The one is like aversion to the taste of a certain substance—the other is like a love for its taste, but a dread of its poisonous quality. Both will lead us to forsake sin: but while the one leads us to do it, because the sin is displeasing to the God whom we love; the other causes us to do it, out of fear to God, whose wrath we dread, but to whose moral character we have no love. The one leads to cheerful, the other to reluctant reformation.—The one produces a hearty, earnest desire after holiness in itself considered; the other, a desire for holiness for the sake of the happiness to which it leads; and it is generally attended with a secret desire that this happiness might be obtained without being holy.

V. Delight in Holiness.—This is a twin grace with *hatred of sin,* and springs from the same temper of heart. While the temper of the heart is the same, objects of opposite moral characters must excite opposite moral affections. Sin and holiness being opposite, the same heart which contemplates the one with dislike and pain, contemplates the other with complacency and delight. That love of complacency, heretofore considered, is a constituent part of this delight in holiness; for the saint loves God, because his attributes and dealings are holy. And he loves Christians, because their characters and conduct are holy. But delight in holiness extends much farther. The saint loves the *worship* of God because it is holy; and the *word* of God because it is holy. And for the same reason, he "delights in the law of God after the inward man." He will approve of all the commands and all the penalties of that law. He will feel that it is right for God to require constant and perfect obedience from all mankind. And he will feel, that in failing to render this continual and complete obedience, he justly deserves the eternal displeasure and curse of God. Nay, he will not only acquiesce in the precepts and penalties of this law; but he will take a satisfaction in doing the duties which it enjoins. He finds that "in keeping the commands of God, there is great reward." He mourns that he serves God so little; and he earnestly desires to serve him better. In a word, he "hungers and thirsts after righteousness."

But this grace has also its counterfeits, against which the reader should take heed. This genuine grace is what is so often called "the love of holiness for holiness' sake." The spurious kind may called (if it be not a solecism,) "the love of holiness for *happiness'* sake." The one is a delight in the *nature* of holiness. The other is only a *desire to gain the profits* of holiness. He who has the former, wishes to be holy, even although it would make him no more happy in this or the coming world. He who has only the latter, would have no desire to be holy, if he did not hope to be made happy by it. And all the while that he is wishing to be holy, he secretly wishes he could be happy without it. And after all, in holiness *itself* he has *no* delight. A man may think he delights in the word of God, while in fact he has no love at all for it. He mistakes *delight* for *interest.* He reads the word of God with interest, it is true; but it is only for the sake of gaining some advantage from it. He feels only an anxiety to learn the way of life, or to obtain some object not so laudable.—And all the time he has no love to the truth which this word of God contains, and no relish for the duties which this word commands. He has no *enjoyment* while he reads; or, if enjoyment he has, it arises from the expectation of private advantage from the perusal.

So of the worship of God. A man may think he takes delight in secret prayer, or in attending public worship: whereas, he only rejoices in the hope that by attention to such services, he shall gain the favour of God, and finally be saved. In the worship *itself* he has no satisfaction; and if it were not for the expected advantage, he would forsake it at once. He attends to it (as a patient does to a disagreeable medicine,) for the sake of future advantage from it. But genuine delight in worship, is a relish for the sacred service. It is like the pleasure which is felt while taking a medicine which is not only salutary to the system, but pleasant to the taste.

So, also, respecting all other duties. A man may think that he takes delight in obeying the law of God, while all his eagerness, and promptitude, and satisfaction, arises not out of the pleasant nature of the service, but out of an expectation of advantage from it. He does it perhaps to be seen of men, and is gladdened by receiving this desired reward. Or, he does it to lay God under obligation to bless and save him; and the expectation of this good, gives him satisfaction while he attends to the tedious service. But genuine delight in God's service, arises from a consideration of the reasonableness and fitness of this service; from love to the Being to whom it is due, and a desire, therefore, to please him; and from that new and peculiar temper of the heart by which this service becomes agreeable. Consequently, this delight in God's service may be found, and doubtless *is* found, where there is no expectation of personal profit from attention to it.

If it needs to be proved that delight in holiness is an unfailing evidence of a saving change of heart, it will be sufficient to remark, 1st. The unregenerate have no delight in holiness: that on the contrary, they have a deep rooted aversion to it, "Because the carnal mind is enmity against God; for it is not subject to the law of God, neither indeed can be." Rom. viii. 7. Consequently, he who loves and delights in holiness, must have been born again. 2d. As religion has its seat in the heart, love of holiness is *holiness itself*, being holiness of heart. 3d. As hatred of sin, and delight in holiness, both arise from the same temper of heart, if the former is evidence of grace, (and we have just seen that it is,) then the other is evidence also.—And for this reason, they both evince the same state of heart. And 4th. *Hatred* of holiness disqualifies us for Heaven; while *delight* in holiness is the very thing that fits us for the enjoyments of that blessed state.

But if it were necessary to furnish proof from Scripture, that delight in holiness is evidence of salvation, a great proportion of that blessed volume might be brought to bear upon the point. But two passages are all that need now be quoted.—"Blessed is the man that feareth the Lord, that *delighteth greatly in his commandments*." Ps. cxii. 1. "Great peace have they which *love thy law*, and nothing shall offend them." Ps. cxix. 165.—To "delight in the commandments," and to "love God's law," evidently signifies to delight in the holiness which they enjoin. And the blessings pronounced in these verses, upon such as have this delight are no less than salvation.

Every real saint will have all the above mentioned affections. Yet, generally speaking, all of them will not be equally strong and constant. In some saints, one affection will be superior; in others, another affection will be superior. And each one, generally, has his prevailing grace—his ruling passion. Hence, that variety of character which prevails among Christians who have, on the whole, an equal attainment in grace. This variety in relation to these Christian affections, is sometimes owing to natural dispositions, sometimes to providential circumstances, and sometimes to the sovereignty of that Spirit which "divideth to every man severally as he will." 1 Cor. xii. 11. In some cases perhaps, some of these graces are scarcely perceptible ; while others are very clearly discerned. Some may be very sensible of love to the brethren, while they are quite at a loss to know whether they have real love to God. Others again may be very sensible of delight in reading the word of God, who are quite at a loss whether they have genuine delight in secret prayer. Some may be very sensible that they hate sin, who are not so sensible that they "hunger and thirst after righteousness." Some may feel at times a full resignation to God's will, who are not so fully satisfied that they love all his perfections. And so it may be respecting other Christian affections. Yet, if a person has one of these affections, he has all of them. But some of them may be so faint in their exercise, as not to be very easily perceived. If, then, a person knows that he has any one of these affections, he may know that he has passed from death unto life.

The reader may think it strange that I say nothing of outward obedience as evidence of saving grace. It is granted that 'the keeping of God's commandments,' and 'the bringing forth of good fruit,' are mentioned in Scripture as evidences of saving grace. 1 John ii. 3—5; Matt. vii. 16—21. But mere *outward* obedience, without right motives, and without a right temper of heart, is not keeping God's commands. All his commands are summed up in love. "Jesus saith unto him, Thou shalt love the Lord thy God with all thy heart, and with all thy soul, and with all thy mind. This is the first and great commandment. And the second is like unto it, Thou shalt love thy neighbour as thyself. *On these two commandments hang all the law and the prophets.*" Matt. xxii. 37—40. All the duties, then, which the law and the prophets enjoin, require love. The commands of God, then, have regard to the heart. It is the temper of the heart with which an action is performed, that gives that action its moral character. A man may be as strict in outward obedience as the Pharisees were, and at the same time be as hypocritical, and thus as far from righteousness, as they. "Except your righteousness shall exceed the righteousness of the Scribes and Pharisees, ye shall in no case enter into the kingdom of Heaven." Matt. v. 20. Mere outward good works, cannot be that "keeping of the commandments," that "bringing forth of good fruits," which the Scriptures declare to be evidence of a saving change of heart.

But although outward good works are not *of themselves*, evidence of saving grace, they are not to be overlooked in the inquiry respecting our spiritual state. Although we have not considered outward obedience as sufficient evidence of a change of heart, we have mentioned as such evidence several affections which lead to good works, and which will not fail to produce them. We have mentioned love, that love on which "all the law and the prophets hang;" Matt. xxii. 37—40: that love which is 'the fulfilling of the law,' Rom. xiii. 10: that love by which "faith *worketh*," Gal. v. 6.—Love prompts to spontaneous obedience. We have mentioned *hatred of sin*. And surely he who hates sin, will abstain from outward acts of sin; consequently will discharge outward duties. And his abstinence from transgression, and consequently his faithfulness in duty, will be just in proportion of his hatred of sin. We have mentioned *delight in holiness:* and he who takes delight in holy duties, will most assuredly discharge them.

He, then, who pays no external obedience to the commands of God, has none of these internal affections. And here, then, is one of the benefits of outward obedience. It is a test by which to try our affections. "Show me thy faith without thy works, and I will show thee my faith *by* my works." James ii. 18. If our supposed religious affections do not lead us to external obedience, they are not those holy affections which are evidence of a change of heart. Outward obedience there may be without regeneration; but regeneration there cannot be without such obedience. "Wo unto you, Scribes and Pharisees, hypocrites! for ye make clean the outside of the cup and of the platter, but within they are full of extortion and excess. Thou blind Pharisee, cleanse first that which is within the cup and the platter, that the outside of them may be clean also." Matt. xxiii. 25, 26. If a man have holy affections, he will have holy conduct. If he be *inwardly* holy, he will be *outwardly* holy. Or, to come nearer to the language of Christ, 'if the inside be clean, the outside will be clean also.' Not that every Christian will be perfectly upright in all his conduct; but that he will be upright in it in *proportion* to his internal piety.

PART II.

HAVING attended to the first inquiry, viz. *What are evidences of a saving change of heart?* we come now to the second inquiry, viz.

Whether we have these evidences?

And here we are entering on the most difficult part of our subject. Hitherto we have been following the unerring guidance of the word of God.—But now we have nothing to secure us from error, but our own perception and judgment. We are not now inquiring, What saith the word of God? but we are inquiring, Whether those holy affections of which the word of God speaks, have any place in our hearts? Our inquiry is not into the meaning of the Bible, but into the feelings of our own bosoms.

A calm and dispassionate state of mind, is the best suited to pursuing an intricate and difficult inquiry. But in this inquiry, difficult and intricate as it is, there is much to agitate and confuse the mind. The vast importance of the inquiry has no small tendency to create this confusion. Earnest wishes on the one hand to find these favourable evidences, and strong fears on the other hand, lest we be found destitute, tend to that state of mind which is least suited to success.

And these desires have no small tendency to warp our judgment. We are very apt to *believe* that true which we *wish* to *have* true. "Passion has a tendency to magnify its object." Our desire to find evidence in our favor has a tendency to swell that evidence in our view, beyond its real extent. The mind naturally dwells more on pleasant than on unpleasant objects. It is therefore inclined to dwell more on evidences *for* than *against* us: the relative consequence is, to magnify the former and diminish the latter.

On the other hand, our *fears* sometimes prevail, and consequently warp our judgment. Knowing that nothing is so fatal as an unfounded hope of salvation, we are almost afraid to take a full look at the favourable side, lest our deceitful hearts should draw us into presumption. We hardly dare think favourably of our case, even when evidence *is* favourable. And some are constitutionally cautious and fearful. And they are the more apt to give way to this distrustful disposition, because they see a natural and prevailing rashness in others, leading them, it is to be feared, to an unfounded and fatal hope of salvation. This self-distrust, though much safer than self-confidence, is yet very hurtful; as it keeps them from hoping, when it is their duty and benefit to hope.

But, other difficulties there are; difficulties growing out of those very affections which are the only evidence of grace. They arise from the short duration, the faintness and mixture of the affections. *Their short duration makes it difficult.* Holy affections, especially when intense, are generally of short continuance. And during their continuance, the mind is not so much at leisure as at other times. It is so occupied as to spend very little or no time in examining these affections during their existence. And the recollection of them is much fainter than the original impression. When, therefore, we call them to remembrance for the purpose of examining their nature, it is always at disadvantage.

Their faintness makes it difficult. Many have but faint holy exercises. And it is difficult to scan with accuracy, what are so dimly perceived; espepecially to ascertain whether they are genuine or spurious affections. Even if they should continue long enough, and the mind had leisure enough for the examination, it would be difficult. But it is still more difficult to examine them by recollection. With many, these affections are so faint that they are led to think they have none at all.

Their mixture makes it difficult. The mixture of these holy affections with unholy ones, is what generally renders it most difficult to ascertain their nature. As no Christians are perfect, all of them have a mixture of good and evil affections. And the difference between the more perfect and imperfect saints, consists in the different proportions of their good and bad exercises. And as the movements of the mind are inconceivably rapid, the transition from the good to the bad is very rapid also. Nay, most of the volitions of the mind may be prompted by a *variety* of motives, some good, some bad. This makes it extremely difficult to discriminate our exercises. When a great proportion of the motives which lead to a volition or action are good, we are apt to think them all good, and therefore, that such a volition or action is perfectly holy. When a great proportion of them are evil, we are apt to think them all bad, and therefore, that such a volition or action is perfectly void of holiness.—No wonder, then, that when piety is low, we should very much doubt whether we have any piety at all.

Such, then, being the difficulties in the way of knowing our own exercises, and therefore, of obtaining *the full assurance of hope*, it must require no ordinary degree of diligence. The Scriptures accordingly command us to "show the same diligence to the full assurance of hope unto the end." Heb. vi. 11. And to "give diligence to make our calling and election sure." 2 Pet. i. 10.

It is hoped, however, that many of the difficulties in the way of obtaining assurance of hope, may be prevented by attending to the following *directions* and *remarks*.

1. *Keep it in view that the heart by nature is* TOTALLY DEPRAVED. The total depravity of the heart should always be our starting point, whenever we would inquire for evidence of saving grace. The doctrine of total depravity being true, the line of division between the sinner and the saint, is drawn between *no* holiness and the *lowest degree* of holiness. For if the sinner has by nature no holiness, when the least and lowest degree of holiness can be found in him, he is no longer a sinner, but a saint. The small degree of holiness in him, must

have been implanted there by regenerating grace. Regeneration is the *beginning* of holiness in the soul. He, then, who has the lowest degree of holy exercise, must be a Christian.

If we suppose the line of division to be drawn any where else than between no holiness and the lowest degree of holiness, all is uncertainty and confusion. If we suppose it to be drawn between some lesser and larger degree of holiness, we must for ever be subject to doubts where it lies; for the Scriptures no where tell us how many degrees of holiness are necessary to constitute us Christians. And if they did, it would be impossible for us to measure those degrees, so as to ascertain with confidence whether we had the requisite number.

But if we suppose the line to be drawn between *no holiness* and the *lowest degree of holiness*, all will be definite and plain. Then to be a Christian, is not to be destitute of all holy affections. Then, if in the midst of our numerous sinful exercises, we can find any that are holy, we have the adequate evidence that we have passed from death unto life; for if we had not been born again, no such holy affections could be found in our heart.

The position, *that the least degree of holiness furnishes evidence of a saving change of heart*, is supported by all those passages of Scripture which prove the doctrine of *total depravity*. Gen vi. 5. "And God saw that the wickedness of man was great in the earth, and that every imagination of the thoughts of his heart was *only evil continually*."

Such is the testimony of God concerning the wicked. *The imaginations of the thoughts of the heart*, signify "the workings of the fancy, the contrivances of the understanding, the purposes, desires, and affections of the whole soul." If, then, in the sinner "every" one of these is "evil," evil *only*, or without mixture of good, and evil *continually*, without cessation, it follows that if any man have the least degree of holiness, he has ceased to be a sinner. The least degree of holiness is therefore full evidence that he is born again.

John v. 42, (said Christ to the unregenerate Jews,) "But I know you, that ye have not the love of God in you." Sinners, then, have no love to God; it follows, therefore, that if a man have the least degree of this love, he is a Christian. That is, the least degree of love to God, is evidence of a change of heart.

Rom. vii. 18, "But I know that in me, that is, in *my flesh*, dwelleth no good thing." By *the flesh*, the apostle evidently means the unsanctified nature, as did Christ when he said, "That which is born of the flesh, is flesh." John iii. 6. Men in an unsanctified state, have no moral goodness in them. They then that possess any goodness or holiness, are not "in the flesh," but *in the spirit*. That is, they are born again. The least degree of holiness, then, is evidence of regeneration.

Rom. viii. 7, 8. "Because the carnal mind is enmity against God; for it is not subject to the law of God, neither indeed can be. So, then, they that are in the flesh cannot please God." "The carnal mind," evidently means the unrenewed heart. If, then, the unrenewed heart is absolute enmity to God, it can have no love to him. It follows, then, that the heart which exercises *any* love to him, is no longer a carnal heart; but a spiritual, a regenerated heart. This unregenerate heart is moreover "not subject to the law of God." The heart, then, that exercises any submission and obedience to God must be a regenerated heart. "They that are in the flesh cannot please God." That is, they that are *unregenerate* cannot please God. But God *is* pleased with holiness. The unregenerate have then no holiness. If, therefore, a man has the least degree of holiness, he is no longer in the flesh, but is born of God. It follows, then, that the least degree of love to God, or submission to his will, nay, the least degree of holiness of any kind, is adequate evidence of a saving change of heart. We have here recited but a small portion of the passages that prove the total depravity of the natural heart. But even these are abundantly sufficient to show that doctrine to be true; and, consequently, that the lowest degree of holy exercise is evidence of a change of heart.

Other passages prove this position more directly. 1 John iv. 7. "Every one that loveth is born of God." Not every one that has *a certain degree* of love, but "every one that loveth;" that is, every one that has *any* love, "is born of God." For if a man has any love at all, it may of a truth be said of him, 'he loveth.' It therefore follows, on the authority of this text, that he is born of God. If, on the contrary, a man may have love and yet not be born of God, because he has not love enough, this passage would not be true; for it says, "*Every one* that loveth is born of God:" whereas, (according to this notion,) some that love are not born of him, because they love not *enough.* The meaning of this passage must then be, that if a man have *any* degree of real holy love to God, to his people, to his word and worship, that man is born again.—The same is proven by 1 John iii. 14. "We know that we have passed from death unto life, because we love the brethren." No *degree* of love is here specified. If we have any affection at all for Christians, "we love the brethren;" and therefore may "know that we have passed from death unto life." The lowest degree of genuine love to Christians, because they are Christians, is sufficient evidence of a change of heart.

The promises and denunciations of the gospel prove the same thing. The gospel promises salvation on condition of the least degree of repentance and faith. Its promise to repentance is, "Repent—so iniquity shall not be your ruin." Ezek. xviii. 30. And he that has the least degree of godly sorrow for sin, *repents.* Its promise to faith is, "Believe on the Lord Jesus Christ, and thou shalt be saved." Acts xvi. 31. And he that has the least degree of faith in Christ, *believes* in him. If, then, the least degree of penitence and faith were not evidences of saving grace, these passages would not be true.

The gospel threatens wrath upon those only who have no holy exercises. Its denunciation in relation to faith is, "He that believeth not shall be damned." Mark xvi. 16. "Believeth not," that is, hath no faith; for if a man have the smallest degree of faith in Christ, it cannot in truth be said of him, that *he believeth not.* He cannot, then, be exposed to this denunciation of wrath. On the contrary, if he have *any* faith, it must be said of him *he believeth;* and therefore he comes under the promise, "he that believeth shall be saved." The same may be said in relation to repentance: the gospel denunciation is, "Except ye repent, ye shall all likewise perish." Luke xiii. 3. If a man has any degree of genuine godly sorrow for sin, it cannot be said in truth of him that he does not repent; it must be affirmed of him that he *does* repent: consequently, he comes under the gospel promise, that "iniquity shall not be his ruin." The lowest degree of faith and repentance, then, is full evidence of saving grace in the heart. In the inquiry, therefore, after evidences of salvation, it should always be kept in view, that the unrenewed heart is totally depraved—that if the heart be not renewed by saving grace, there is no moral good in it; consequently, if any good can be found in it, that heart has been regenerated.

2. *Look principally to the nature, and not to the number or strength of the heart's exercises.* It is the *quality*, and not the *quantity* of our affections, which decides the question respecting our spiritual state. We should therefore fear, not that we have not *enough* religious affections, but that we have not those of the *right kind.* If our exercises are spurious, though we have ever so many, and ever so strong ones, we are none the better. But if they are genuine, be they ever so faint and few, still we are safe; for they are full evidence of a saving change of heart. As the unregenerate have no

holiness, the inquiry is, whether in our hearts holiness is *begun;* not how far it has *progressed.*—This beginning is regeneration. And be it ever so small, still it *is* a beginning.

Some of my readers may think that I have here opened a wide door for the entrance of self-deception. As the unregenerate are apt to think they have some moral goodness in them, it may be thought that the foregoing remarks will have a tendency to encourage them in a false hope. But shall the truth be suppressed, lest some should "wrest it unto their own destruction?" If it be true, that the lowest degree of holy exercises of heart, is full proof of a saving change, then it ought to be known, and believed: and to hold up an opposite idea would be wrong. God authorises no suppression of the truth, nor publication of falsehood in relation to religion, out of supposed expediency. Nor does the truth have any tendency to mislead. And as the position here taken has been proven to be the truth, it ought not to be objected to, because it will lead to self-deception.

But I apprehend that some do suppress this truth out of expediency. When they describe the holy affections, it is as they are in their fullest and most perfect exercise. When they describe the Christian, it is a saint of very great attainments in holiness. In pointing out the evidences of a change of heart, they seem to be telling what a Christian *ought to be*, to meet the full acceptance of God, not what he *must be*, to have promise of saving grace. And they seem to set the standard thus high, in order to keep all from hoping who have not very high attainments in religion: to keep those who have but few and faint holy exercises, from believing that they have passed from death unto life. They seem to aim at making it more difficult to obtain a hope in Christ, lest some should hope who have no right to hope. But this is not the guard which they should set up against self-deception; for it is not the guard of truth. It is not a suitable guard, moreover, because it keeps many real saints from hoping in the Lord. There are very many real Christians, whose affections are very low; indeed, there are very few whose affections come up to this high standard; consequently, they will be kept down in doubt and darkness. This setting the standard thus high, will do more to keep the Christian from the hope which he *ought* to have, than it will to keep the sinner from the hope which he ought *not* to have. From some cause or other, among those who are led to inquire whether they have met with a saving change, there prevails a very general opinion, that holy affections must be quite strong and ardent, or we are still in the way of sin and condemnation. And probably it is this wrong maxim, principally, which keeps so many Christians from a cheering hope in the mercy of the Lord. And those writers who set the standard thus high, confirm this wrong maxim, and increase the evil that results from it. While the trembling and doubting Christian should be the special object of their kind and consoling attention, they are confirming his doubts, and increasing his distress.

Nor is this the most effectual guard against a false hope. It does not give the sinner a true test of moral character. Consequently, all examinations by it are lost. The danger of self-deception lies not, in not having a sufficient quantity of exercises; but in not having exercises of a right kind. And the examination should be directed to the place where the danger lies; not to the place where it does not lie. To keep the sinner from self-deception, then, he must be made to look to the *nature*, instead of the *degree* of his affections. And his examinations, if thorough and candid, will terminate in a knowledge of his spiritual state. There is something definite in the inquiry, whether he have *any* holy affections or not? But the inquiry, whether he have *enough* holy affections to constitute him a Christian, is perfectly indefinite.—Even if it were true, that a considerable strength and ardour of affection, were necessary to prove a change of heart, still, the question would be very indefinite, because the precise degree necessary, is not known. And even if the Scriptures did specify how much of every kind of Christian affections must be felt, to secure salvation, we should find it very difficult to measure our own, so as to know whether we came up to the standard or not. It is evident, then, that to know whether we have passed from death unto life, or not, we must look to the *nature*, rather than to the *strength* and *number* of our religious affections. And it is also evident, that if we confine ourselves to the nature of these affections, we shall avoid a vast deal of that difficulty which seems to lie in the way of the full assurance of hope.

3. *To obviate the difficulty arising from the* SHORT DURATION *of religious exercises, consider*

the GENERAL TENOUR *of them.* For instance, as it is difficult to investigate a single transient emotion of love to God, we should consider our love to him in general. We should seize on a course or succession of these emotions, as we recollect them to have risen in our minds during a given time.—A number of them combined, will assume a complexion and character, which we can more closely discern, and more accurately discriminate. So of our love to the saints; so of our hatred to sin; so of our hungering and thirsting after righteousness; so of our resignation; and so of all our other religious affections. If the heart puts forth these affections at one time, it will continue to put them forth, though with longer or shorter intervals.—And although many of the individual emotions can not be called to recollection, yet enough of them can, to form an aggregate for examination: as when viewing a distant landscape, a single separate habitation scarcely can be seen; whereas, a collection of them together, in a village, is easily discerned. And one transient affection can be more easily counterfeited,than a continued train of them: so that in two respects, it is safer to examine each affection in the aggregate. And if a large number of affections of one kind, afford more evidence of salvation than a few of them, still higher will be the evidence derived from a consideration of all the gracious affections together.

4. *To obviate the difficulty arising from the faintness of religious exercises, strive to have stronger ones.* Every one should have that ardent, vigorous love to God, that he cannot but know that he

loves him; and therefore, that he is born of him.—He should feel such delight in the character and company of saints, as to know that he "loves the brethren," and therefore, is "passed from death unto life." He should have such a deep, godly sorrow for sin, as shall make it evident that he has the repentance which is unto salvation. He should have such entire, cheerful, and constant submission to God's will, as cannot leave it doubtful whether he has resignation. And he should have that hungering and thirsting after holiness, which will render it evident that he delights in holiness. Such full exercises all *can* have, and *ought* to have. And if they did but have them, their nature would be evident. They would at once appear to be the offspring of nothing less than regenerating grace.

5. *To obviate the difficulty arising from the* MIXTURE *of holy with unholy affections, take special care to distinguish between them, and consider them apart.* Try to separate the good from the bad, and consider the nature of the good ones by themselves. And let your inquiry be, not how many evil affections you have? but whether you have any good affections mingled with your evil ones? For if in the multitude of your affections, the most of which are unholy, you can find any that are holy, these will furnish the adequate evidence that you are born again.

'But I show unto you a more excellent way.'—It is to lessen the proportion of evil affections, and increase the proportion of those that are holy.—This, also, we *can* do, and *ought* to do. And if there were a less proportion of evil affections mingled with our good ones, how much easier would it be to examine them; and thus gain assurance that we "have passed from death unto life."

From the foregoing remarks on the *short duration*, *faintness*, and *mixture* of our affections, it must be evident, that *faithfulness in duty*, is of great service in obtaining the full assurance of hope. If we were more faithful, our holy exercises would be more frequent, consequently their aggregate would be much greater; and would therefore, be the easier to examine, and afford the fuller proof of a saving change of heart. If we were more faithful, our religious affections would also be much more full and ardent; consequently, their moral character would be more prominent; and on this account also, they would be more easily examined, and afford the fuller proof of an interest in the saving grace of God. If we were more faithful too, the proportion of our holy, above our *un*-holy affections, would also be much greater; and would, therefore, present more plain and convincing testimony that we had passed from death unto life.

That faithfulness in duty will increase our holy exercises, is evident. Even the discharge of outward duties, will have this tendency. It is evident that while we are engaged in divine worship, we shall have a different current of thoughts and feelings, from what we should, if we were then employed in our worldly affairs. Our thoughts and affections will generally be in conformity to our present employment. The more, then, we are employed in holy duties, the more holy contemplations and affections shall we have.

9 *

But faithfulness in duty, has regard, not only to the external conduct, but to the internal workings of the soul. To be faithful in duty, we must watch over the heart, guard it from evil thoughts and affections, and strive to excite it to those that are holy. "We should keep our hearts with all diligence, knowing that out of them may be the issues of life." Prov. iv. 23. Nor will such watchfulness be in vain. It will secure much more holiness of heart. And thus it will do much to obviate the difficulty arising from the *short duration* and the *mixture* of our affections.

But such faithfulness in duty, will increase not only the number, but the *strength* of our holy affections. And thus it will obviate the difficulty arising from the *faintness* of our exercises. It will be found from experience, that the more constant and strict we are in any duty, the more delight we have in it; and of course, the more perfect are our affections while discharging it. He that improves his five talents, gains other five talents. Matt. xxv. 16. Christians "purify their souls by obeying the truth." 1 Pet. i. 22. The more faithful they are, then, in obedience, the more pure they will become: that is, the stronger and more numerous will be their holy affections.

And faithfulness in duty, secures the influence of the Spirit. 'The more fruit of godliness we bear, the more will God purge us by his Spirit, that we may bring forth *still* more fruit.' John xv. 2. He that improved his five talents, not only gained five more, but had still another given him, that he might "have abundance." Matt. xxv. 29. While unfaithfulness tends on the other hand to quench the influence of the Spirit, and to grieve him away: and on this account we are cautioned against neglect of duty. It is plain, then, that the more faithful we are in duty, the more of the Spirit's influence we shall enjoy; and therefore the more easy it will be for us to ascertain, whether we are born again.

There is yet another respect in which faithfulness in duty renders it more easy for us to know our spiritual state. It gives us a better opportunity to see whether our hearts "really relish the holy duties of religion." The more constantly we attend to secret prayer, the more opportunities we have to judge whether we really love these devotions of the closet. The more strictly we attend on the public worship of God, the more we can see whether we delight in the duties of his house; and therefore, the better we can judge, whether we have a temper of heart that would delight in the worship that is paid by saints in light. The more we do to advance the cause of Christ, and to save the souls of sinners, the better we can judge whether we do these things out of selfish motives, or out of love to Christ and benevolence to man. In short, the more we engage in the things of religion, the better we can judge whether we have a love for holiness; and, therefore, whether we have passed from death unto life.

The more then we are in doubt respecting our spiritual state, the more faithful on this account we ought to be in duty. But those who are doubting, are apt to reason to the reverse of this. They are apt to think there is not so much need of their being faithful, as there would be, if they knew they were Christians. They say within themselves, "If I knew I were a Christian, I should not dare to omit this and that duty. But since I have very little evidence that I am a real saint, it is not so important for me to be so very strict in my conduct."—And Satan takes opportunity, from this their state of mind, to insinuate to them, that as they are not Christians, it is all hypocrisy for them to be so attentive to religious duties. Thus by their own false reasoning, and by the temptations of Satan, they are seduced into greater looseness of life, and thus are carried into greater and greater darkness and doubt. Whereas, if they did but strictly attend to every Christian duty, they would soon be rejoicing in "a good hope through grace."

These directions to faithfulness in duty, accord with those given by the apostle Peter on this subject. He says, "And besides this, giving all diligence, add to your faith, virtue; and to virtue, knowledge; and to knowledge, temperance; and to temperance, patience; and to patience, godliness; and to godliness, brotherly kindness; and to brotherly kindness, charity. For if these things be in you, and abound, they make you that, ye be neither barren nor unfruitful in the knowledge of our Lord Jesus Christ. But he that lacketh these things is blind, and cannot see afar off, and hath forgotten that he was purged from his old sins.—*Wherefore the rather, brethren, give diligence to make your calling and election sure:* for if ye do these things, ye shall never fall." 2 Pet. i. 5—10. A bare look at the continued and intimate connexion of this whole passage, will convince us, that the apostle here urges us to make our calling and election sure, by *adding to our faith, virtue, knowledge, temperance, patience, godliness, brotherly kindness, and charity.* The amount of it is, he urges us to the faithful discharge of the whole round of Christian duties, as the means of attaining the full assurance of hope.

If the foregoing directions were strictly followed, much of the difficulty in the way of obtaining a hope of salvation, would be thereby prevented.—But to the attainment of the *full assurance* of hope, two things more are necessary. They are *promptness* and *perseverance.* It is the want of these things which keeps so many Christians in doubt, respecting their spiritual state. They are irresolute, and dilatory in regard to self-examination; or if for a time they pursue the examination with promptness, they do not persevere till they perfect it. If Christians were to manifest as much want of promptness and perseverance in their temporal, as in their spiritual concerns, they would become the butt of ridicule and reproach. But they do not. If any doubt arises respecting their title to their farms, they are all eagerness in searching the records, and n looking up testimony in the case. They delay not a day, lest death should deprive them of their necessary testimony. But while their title to a 'heavenly inheritance' is in vast uncertainty, they delay to search into it; or if they do at all examine their title, it is with as little earnestness and constancy, as if this inheritance were of little or no importance. But this inheritance, according to the Saviour's valuation, is of more importance than all the treasures on earth. How much more anxious should we, then, be respecting it; and how much more prompt and persevering should we be to secure this, than a title to an earthly possession?

It is important, that our self-examination should be attended to *without delay.* If we put it off today, to-morrow death may meet us unprepared; or some other incident may intervene to prevent our attention to it hereafter. And that dilatory spirit which leads us to delay it *to-day*, will be just as apt to lead us to delay it *to-morrow.*

It is important that the examination should be attended to with *earnestness* and *vigour.* A faint and fluctuating attention to it, will leave the matter in as much uncertainty as ever.

It is important that the examination should be *constant* and *persevering*, until we ascertain whether we are Christians or not. If the examination be broken off by frequent and long interruptions, all the labour is lost. What was done at one time is mostly, if not wholly forgotten, after such interruptions; and the whole ground of inquiry needs again to be gone over. How should we conduct, if we were at a loss whether a certain and valuable treasure were in our possession or not? Should we only cast such a careless look about the house, when accidentally passing over it, as would leave us in almost as much uncertainty as ever respecting it? And after that should we go about other concerns, till we had entirely forgotten in what parts of the house we had looked for it? No, at such folly we should either laugh or frown. But such is the conduct of many respecting their evidences of grace. When they examine themselves, they do it so carelessly, that they are scarcely the wiser for the search. They moreover examine but a small portion of the ground at once; and the work is so long interrupted, that when they begin the work again, they have forgotten what portion was before examined. And so perhaps the same portion is often examined, while the rest are not examined at all.—How much greater the folly of conducting thus in *spiritual*, than in *temporal* concerns.

If inquiring whether we possessed some precious treasure or not, we should search not only every apartment of our house, but every trunk and drawer in it; and we should make the search so thorough, that when we left each apartment, we should know whether the treasure were in it; and thus go through our whole habitation, nor rest till we knew whether this treasure were ours. With how much greater promptitude and perseverance, should we search then every apartment of the soul, to see if we can find in it 'the pearl of great price.' For instance, we should examine our *love* in all its various features, to ascertain whether it be genuine or spurious, then our *humility*, then our *resignation;* and so on, examining all our affections, one by one. And we should be careful to examine them so thoroughly, that we should not need to repeat the examination. We should continue our research without interruption, till we have gone through with every affection which has any relation to saving grace. Self-examination should not be left to fill up a leisure hour. We should make a *business* of it. We should make it our *first concern*, and feel that whatever else may be neglected, ***this must not.*** Let the self deceived sinner attend thus to the work, and he will find himself "in the gall of bitterness, and bonds of iniquity." Let the doubting saint attend to it thus, and he will **ATTAIN THE FULL ASSURANCE OF HOPE.**

CHAPTER IV.

SHOWING THE IMPORTANCE OF OBTAINING THE FULL ASSURANCE OF HOPE.

THE full assurance of hope, though a *possible*, is yet a *rare* attainment. Many think they have it, while it is to be feared they have nothing but presumption. They are confident that they are Christians, while they are "in the gall of bitterness, and bonds of iniquity." And perhaps there are not a few real Christians, who are confident of salvation, but whose confidence is not founded on the real and only evidences of grace. They have only stumbled on a right conclusion respecting their state.—They have guessed with confidence, and have happened to guess right. But probably, by far the greater part of Christians are in much doubt respecting their spiritual condition. Many believing that full assurance is not attainable, have not attempted to reach it. And others who have believed it attainable, have failed from other causes.—Some fail because they mistake in relation to what are evidences of grace. They suppose some things necessary to a state of grace, which are not necessary; and because they have them not, they remain in doubt: or, they have not distinctly learned what are evidences of grace; and therefore, though they have holy affections, they do not consider them as proof of their gracious state. Others, again, who have sufficient information respecting what the evidences are, neglect self-examination, and thus remain in doubt. Others, again, who know the proper evidences, and who are not entirely deficient in self-examination, fail through the *faintness* and *mixture* of their exercises. They neither practice that faithfulness which would obviate these difficulties, nor search with sufficient diligence to discriminate the nature of their faint and mixed affections. We have said, the best way to obviate these difficulties, is to be very faithful in duty. Few are thus faithful; and through a want of this faithfulness, many, very many, fail of the full assurance of hope. Some have peculiar temptations to encounter; and others are of a gloomy and doubting temperament. And these things often contribute to their failure of this desirable attainment.

As, then, so many Christians fail of obtaining assurance of hope, they need to be excited to it.—Those readers who have been discouraged from attempting to attain it, by the opinion that all their attempts would be unavailing, have had their discouragements removed, we hope, by perusing the foregoing pages. But they, and others, will need additional excitement. This excitement it is proposed now to present, by showing *the importance of attaining the full assurance of hope.*

It is important to attain this assurance,

I. Because *God requires us to have it.* As we have seen under the fourth proof, that the full assurance of faith is attainable, God frequently commands it. By the mouth of the apostle Paul, he says: "Examine yourselves whether ye be in the faith: *prove* your own selves. *Know ye not*, your own selves, how that Jesus Christ is in you, except ye be reprobates? 2 Cor. xiii. 5. Again he says,

"And we desire that every one of you do show the same diligence unto the full assurance of hope."— Heb. vi. 11. And by the mouth of another apostle he says, "Give diligence to make your calling and election sure." 2 Pet. i. 10. God, then, commands us to have the assurance of hope; and what he commands us, we should do without gainsaying, whether we have any particular benefit arising from it or not. It is enough that God has commanded it. Our province in such cases, is implicit obedience; and were there no other reason for attaining the full assurance of hope, this would be sufficient. The command of God looks down every objection, and makes it of the utmost importance that the full assurance of hope should be attained.

But it is important that it should be attained,

II. *Because our endeavours will secure us against self-deception; consequently, against the danger of eternal perdition.* All who do not know that they are Christians, do not know but they are yet "in the gall of bitterness, and bonds of iniquity." We have reason to believe, from what the Scriptures say on the subject, that many who hope they are saints, are still in sin, and thus as much exposed as ever to the eternal wrath of God. While, therefore, we have not assurance of our salvation, how much reason we have to fear, that 'while we think we stand, we are ready to fall;' that we have only 'the lamp of profession without the oil of grace;' that we have 'gone to the wedding without the wedding garment;' that though we 'eat and drink in Christ's presence, nay, though we teach and prophecy in his name, and even cast out devils,' nevertheless, he will at length say to us, "I *never* knew you." What more dangerous state then, can a man be in, than to hope he is a Christian while he is yet in his sins? He believes himself on the way to heaven, while passing rapidly down to hell.—While this delusive hope continues, he is in far greater danger than careless sinners. They feel that their state is unsafe. There is hope, therefore, that the warnings of the gospel will awaken them; at least, that the approach of danger will alarm them. But what will alarm him who hopes he has made his peace with God already? But while we have hope, and yet not the *full assurance* of hope, we know not but this is our condition. We know not but that we have just enough of this delusive hope, to keep us along in self-security, till the day of grace is gone for ever. The frail raft may be just strong enough to bear a man along, where the water is shallow and still; and where, therefore, if it failed him, he might easily escape to the shore. But if it reaches the current and the depth of the stream, it will be speedily torn asunder, and leave him to perish without remedy. All it avails him, is to bear him into perdition. So this uncertain hope may be barely sufficient to buoy us up in seeming safety, until we reach the current of death, and then abandon us to final despair. But from all this danger, a faithful attempt to obtain the full assurance of hope, would effectually deliver us. If *sinners*, the attempt would show us our real condition of exposure to the wrath of God; and probably arouse us to escape from it. If *saints*, it would show us that our salvation was secure. How important on this account then, that we 'give diligence to make our calling and election sure.'

III. It is important, *because it prevents our present pain, and promotes our present enjoyment.* In all things, suspense and doubt are painful; and they are distressing in proportion to the amount of interest supposed to be involved. How painful must they be then, where the infinite and eternal interest of the soul is rightly apprehended, and is found to be in uncertainty. If uncertainty respecting a small amount of property will create such anxiety and pain, what should be felt when in doubt respecting the soul, for whose loss the world could not compensate? If a trial at law, involving character or interest, excite so much anxiety, and if uncertainty respecting its decision should cause so much pain; what agony should be felt when in doubt, how the 'Judge of quick and dead' will decide at last on our character and destiny? whether he will say, "Come ye blessed of my Father, inherit the kingdom prepared for you from the foundation of the world:" or whether he will say, "Depart ye cursed, into everlasting fire, prepared for the devil and his angels." But such is the distressing uncertainty which hangs over the prospect of him who has not 'made his calling and election sure.' He knows not whether he is on the way to heaven, or on the way to hell; and in consequence of this doubt, how much painful anxiety might he endure. But all this distress the attainment of assurance will prevent. They who are assured of their salvation, are freed from such fearful solicitude.

Nor is this all: assurance not only *prevents much pain*, but *produces much pleasure*. There is an indescribable delight in contemplating our safety in the midst of surrounding dangers. What, then, must be the satisfaction of contemplating perfect safety from the gathering storm of divine indignation. Still greater is the delight in contemplating our *escape* from danger that once threatened us.—We gaze upon the danger and the escape with wonder, with gratitude and joy. What unspeakable satisfaction must *he* then feel, who sees himself to be safe from the yawning gulf which lately was "moved from beneath to meet him at his coming."

There is, moreover, a very great satisfaction derived from the anticipation of good to come. This satisfaction will be great in proportion to the confidence with which we hope for this good; and the full assurance of hope is the highest confidence.—This satisfaction will be great, too, in proportion to the supposed value of the good in expectance; and the object of the Christian's hope is infinite, eternal. He, therefore, who has the full assurance of a glorious immortality, has anticipations most joyous and delightful. As, then, the full assurance of hope prevents so much painful anxiety, and so much promotes the Christian's enjoyment, how important that we strive to attain it.

IV. It is important, *because the want of it* prevents, *and the* possession *of it* promotes, *our faithfulness in duty*. It is the want of assurance that keeps many Christians from making a public profession of religion, coming to the table of the Lord, and devoting their children to God in baptism.

True, it is not necessary that they have assurance before they proceed to these duties. If they have but a prevailing comfortable hope, they should not delay. But many there are who do delay, because they have yet some doubts respecting their spiritual state. It is, therefore, important that they should remove their doubts: these doubts are sinful in *themselves.* And if they keep them from professing religion, they have a *double sinfulness.* How important, then, that these doubts should be removed! To doubt is one sin; to neglect owning Christ before men, is another sin. The first should be removed, that the other may be prevented.

Doubts respecting our spiritual state, tend to chill our holy affections, and to paralyze the spiritual energies of our souls. How often does an occasional cloud of darkness keep the saint from his closet, from the prayer meeting, or from the religious conference! How often does it keep him from warning his fellow sinners to flee from the wrath to come; and from encouraging and comforting his fellow saint? Who can tell, then, how much a *constant* uncertainty respecting his state, retards him in the duties which he does perform; and from how many duties it effectually withholds him? Under the influence of this uncertainty, in gratitude, his heart faints; in praise, his voice faulters. In fine, this uncertainty spreads a deadening influence over all his affections and conduct. And Satan undoubtedly plies his temptations most furiously, with those Christians who have the least hope. What Christian has not observed that when he was in the most darkness, he was most assaulted with "the fiery darts of the wicked." At such times Satan strives, and often with too much success, to convince the Christian, that it is of no use for him to be so strict in duty; nay, that as he is not a Christian, all such strictness in him is nothing but hypocrisy. Hence it is, that we see those Christians most slack in duty, who doubt most respecting their spiritual state.

Uncertainty respecting his spiritual state, will keep him from faithfulness in duty, not only by *influencing his feelings and resolutions*, but also by *occupying his attention.* While occupied with his doubts, he cannot be occupied with duty. While dwelling on his darkness and fears, he cannot be breathing forth those holy and devout affections, nor be employed in those holy duties which God has commanded. This will check his faithfulness, especially in the duty of seeking the prosperity ot Zion, and the salvation of sinners. Who will engage heartily and constantly in this important duty, while doubting whether 'he has any part or lot in this matter?' It is important, then, that our calling and election be made sure, so that when we are discharging our duty, our minds need not be called away to the inquiry, whether we have any share in the saving grace of God.

But while doubt tends to hinder our faithfulness, hope, on the contrary, tends to promote it. And the stronger the hope, the more powerful its influence. Consequently, other things being equal, the more hope we have, the more faithful we shall be. How powerful, then, must be the exciting influence of a *full assurance* of hope?

Some speak as if they thought that assurance would lead to unfaithfulness in duty. They insinuate, that if a man knew he was safe, he would rest satisfied with his attainments, and thus grow slack in duty. But they confound *assurance of hope*, with *perfection in duty*. Yet they are perfectly distinct: nor are they inseparable attendants. He who has an assured hope of heaven, will, nevertheless, feel, that he comes far short of duty. Nor will he feel any more contented with his imperfection in duty, because he is certain of salvation. No, he will be less so. The more hope he has of heaven, the more he will 'hunger and thirst after righteousness.' Such is the very tendency of saving grace. And if a man should be contented with his attainments in holiness, merely because he felt confident of salvation, this very circumstance would be sufficient proof, that his confidence was presumption, and that his soul was a stranger to the grace of God.

That the full assurance of hope promotes faithfulness in duty, we learn from the word of God.—Said the apostle, 1 John iii. 2, 3, "But we *know* that when he shall appear, we shall be like him; for we shall see him as he is. And every man that hath this hope in him, purifyeth himself, even as he is pure." Here is not only hope, but the full assurance of hope. "We *know*," says the apostle.—'We know we shall see God in heaven; and that we shall be *like* him, perfectly holy.' Here, then, is the highest assurance of salvation. Here, too, we are told what is the tendency of this assurance. "He that hath this hope," that is, this assured expectation of seeing God, and being like him in heaven; "he that hath this hope, purifieth himself, even as he is pure." Assurance leads to progressive sanctification.

Peter calls this hope "lively;" 1 Pet. i. 3.—That is, a *living*, *active* hope, because it prompts to activity, in the service of God. And if the degree of it, which is usually attained in this life, will prompt to obedience, much more will the full assurance of it do so.

In our spiritual warfare, the Scriptures tell us to put on for a helmet, "the hope of salvation." 1 Thess. v. 8. But why should hope make a part of our spiritual armour? Plainly, because hope inspires courage. It prevents our shrinking from duty, through fear. It fires us forward in the conflict, by the assurance that we shall come off "conquerors, and more than conquerors, through Christ that hath loved us." From the Scriptures, then, it is evident that assurance leads to faithfulness.—The same is evident from the nature of hope itself. We have seen that the want of it, discourages the Christian, exposes him to temptation, and in several ways leads him to be lax in duty. The possession of it, must, therefore, have an opposite influence. It must lead to faithfulness in duty. The apostle tells us, that the goodness of God leads to repentance: that is, a view of his kindness and mercy toward us, will excite in us a sorrow for our transgressions of his law. And the more hope we have of salvation, the deeper sense we shall have of the goodness of God; consequently, the more repentance we shall exercise over our past iniquities; and thence, the more we shall be kept from repeating them. Hope in God's mercy, excites gratitude and love to him. And these will inevitably prompt to holy obedience. And they will be invariably attended by other holy affections, which will also excite to duty. Hope in the final grace of God, will, moreover, promote our confidence in God; consequently, will lead to a holy fortitude and courage in his service. The more hope we have, then, the more ardent and constant will be our holy affections, and the more faithful shall we be in the way of duty.

And what is the testimony of observation and experience on the subject? It coincides with the declarations of Scripture, and the conclusions of reason. Facts declare, that those who have the fullest well grounded hope of salvation, ordinarily render the most faithful obedience unto God.

Thus the *want* of assurance *prevents*, and the *possession* of it, *promotes* our faithfulness in vital and practical godliness. And in this way, assurance produces a threefold benefit. *It glorifies God; it benefits ourselves; and conduces to the salvation of sinners.*

It glorifies God. It encourages saints to confess Christ before men, in a public profession of religion; and thus God is glorified. It awakens saints to more thanksgiving; and *thus* God is glorified. "Whoso offereth praise, glorifieth me," said God, by the Psalmist. It leads saints to more strict obedience to the divine commands; and *thus* God is more particularly glorified. Said Christ, "Herein is my Father glorified, that ye bear much fruit." And when saints are faithful in duty, their fellow-saints rejoice, and praise God for it; and even the wicked are constrained to confess it "manifest, that their deeds are wrought in God:" and thus it causes others to glorify God. Hence, says Christ, "Let your light so shine before men, that they may see your good works, and glorify your Father which is in heaven."

Full assurance of hope, by leading to faithfulness in duty, *benefits ourselves.* "Godliness is profitable unto all things." "Godliness is great gain." The more vital and practical godliness we have, then, the greater our gain. The gains of godliness, have respect both to the *present* and the *coming* world. The Psalmist tells us, that "IN keeping the commands of God, there is great reward." Holy affections, are delightful affections. Holy duties, give great enjoyment. We shall be happy then, in proportion to the amount of our fervour in holy affections, and our faithfulness in holy obedience. And here is an enjoyment arising from assurance, distinct from that arising from the contemplation of our safety in the midst of surrounding dangers, and the anticipation of future felicity; as mentioned in our third reason, why it is important that the full assurance of hope should be attained.

And from what Scripture says, of the different degrees of reward among the righteous, we have considerable reason to conclude, that they are rewarded hereafter, according to their faithfulness in this life. In *proportion* to their faithfulness, but not *for* it. And if so, while the full assurance of hope, is promoting our faithfulness here, it greatly increases our happiness hereafter.

Full assurance of hope, *promotes the salvation of sinners.* Sinners, seeing our doubts and fears respecting our salvation, suppose if they should seek it, they must remain in the same uncertainty, respecting their spiritual state; and thus they are discouraged from striving to attain eternal life.—While, if we had assurance of salvation, they would conclude that if they sought salvation, they also would know whether they had passed from death unto life: and therefore they would be encouraged to strive and attain it by repentance and faith.

Doubts, respecting our spiritual state, keep us back from warning the wicked to flee from the wrath which is to come. Whereas, the full assurance of hope, will encourage us to warn them the more faithfully. And the more they are warned, the more reason we have to hope they will be saved. But assurance of hope, has a general tendency to invigorate piety. And the more zeal we have in the cause of Christ, the more in various ways, shall we be excited to promote the salvation of sinners. Especially, the more shall we pray for their salvation.

And assurance prompts, we have seen, to more zeal and diligence in duty. And the more faithful sinners see us to be, the more will they be constrained to believe there is a reality in religion; and thus the more will their conscience urge them to obtain it. Hence, said Christ, "Let your light so shine before men, that they may see your good works, and glorify your Father who is in heaven."

Since, then, God commands us to have the full assurance of hope; since this assurance secures us against the fatal danger of a false hope; since it prevents much present pain, and produces much present enjoyment; since the want of it, keeps the saint back from many important duties; and since by prompting to faithfulness in duty, it so much promotes the glory of God, our own spiritual welfare, and sinners' salvation, how important that this assurance should be attained. May God give full efficacy to these motives. Through their influence, may the reader be led to "make his calling and election sure."

THE END.

APPENDIX.

CONTAINING

SOME REMARKS ON THE NATURE

OF

SPIRITUAL DARKNESS,

TOGETHER WITH SOME

DIRECTIONS TO SAINTS

WHO ARE LABOURING UNDER IT.

WHEN the saint is first brought "from darkness unto light," (if his exercises are clear,) he imagines that his trials and troubles, are forever over. Contemplating the awful misery from which he has escaped, and contrasting it with the infinite blessedness which he has just won, he is overwhelmed with adoration, gratitude, and joy. Completely occupied for a while with these things, he is unmindful of the remains of corruption, which still have a place in his heart. Indeed, while by his new, happy condition, his heart is called forth in such vigorous holy exercises, this corruption seems to relent; or rather, to lie dormant in the soul. In this state, he confidently supposes, that his conflict with sin and sorrow, is done. He expects that the same cheering sunshine will beam with unclouded brightness on his soul; that the fire of divine love will always burn with the same glowing strength; and that he shall always have the same fervent zeal, to glorify his God and Redeemer. Tell him that clouds and darkness often overspread the Christian sky, that coldness and languor often invade his soul; tell him of the much corruption which remains in the renovated heart, and of the painful warfare which he has to wage with sin through life, and he believes not what you say, or he knows not what you mean. But what he could not believe, or could not understand from the declarations of others, as it too often happens, he is soon brought to know from his own sad experience. Soon his love languishes, his zeal flags, evil thoughts and affections arise in his soul; consequently, his mind is overclouded with thick and painful darkness. Lucid intervals again return, and dark seasons again succeed them. And he continues for a while, rising and relapsing, hoping and fearing. At first he supposes perhaps that no others ever experience such trials; but on inquiry he finds, "There hath no temptation taken him, but such as is common to man." 1 Cor. x. 13. He finds, that generally the Christian's day is made up of alternate sunshine and shade. He finds, that the Christian's path leads not only over many a Pisgah, from whose summit he views the promised land; but that it leads also through many dreary vallies, in which his heavenward prospect is almost intercepted.

Such is the experience of Christians *generally*, but not *invariably*. Nor is it ever *necessary*.— Some Christians have continual and increasing light and comfort, and have never experienced this darkness and distress of which we have been speaking. The Scriptures declare the "path of the just" to be "as the shining light, that shineth more and more unto the perfect day." Prov. iv.18. The Scriptures require a constant increase of Christian graces, censure such as fail of it, and commend such as do grow in grace. It is not necessary, then, for the young convert to grow cold and stupid. On the contrary, he ought to grow more ardent and faithful, and thereby, more happy in the Lord.

Yet, many experienced Christians suppose, because this darkness has befallen them, and many of their fellow saints, it must befall every saint. They, therefore, think it necessary to warn the young convert, that he must endure it. And by this means they often occasion a great deal of needless, distressing and hurtful discouragement to him. It is to be feared, that by this means, many a young convert has been discouraged into that darkness, from which he might else have escaped. He should be told indeed that he is in *danger* of such darkness; but not that he *must of necessity* endure it. On the contrary, he should be told that it is not necessary; that by due faithfulness, he may and ought to avoid it. And it is especially important, that the young convert should be particularly faithful, to secure himself from relapsing into sin and distress; for, if for a while he habituates himself to faithfulness in duty, he will acquire a kind of spiritual stability, which renders it less probable that he will afterwards slide into stupidity, and thereby, into spiritual darkness.

But saints are subject to spiritual darkness in

every stage of their Christian course. They are subject to it after ever so long a course of faithfulness and enjoyment. And sometimes the darkness endured by the faithful saint, is long and distressing. And it is *this* darkness, it is the darkness peculiar to those who have for a considerable time enjoyed the light of God's countenance, that I now propose to consider.

Spiritual darkness is somewhat allied to backsliding, though essentially distinct from it. Darkness is generally occasioned by backsliding. But the one is not generally in proportion to the other. A very small departure from duty, may sometimes occasion the saint a vast deal of spiritual distress.—While in other cases, the saint may wander far, and yet have little or no concern respecting his departure.

Spiritual darkness, is spiritual distress. And this distress is occasioned by several things.—Much of it is occasioned by *desertion*, or the withdrawment of the influence of the holy Comforter, and the interruption of communion with God. In prospect of this, the saint cries out, "Cast me not from thy presence, and take not thy holy Spirit from me." Ps. li. 11. And when God no longer communes with him from off the mercy-seat, he says, "O that I might come, even to his seat."—Job xxiii. 3.

Much of this distress is also occasioned by doubts and fears. Generally when the saint is much depressed, the clouds that hang around him obscure his evidences of grace, bring him to doubt, if not to despair. And any fear respecting our salvation, may well occasion a painful anxiety. Much of it is also occasioned by the loss of that joy which was experienced in the full exercise of godliness; together with self-reproach for neglect of duty: all of which are sufficient to cause the utmost distress.

Much of this distress, is occasioned by what is generally called *hardness of heart.* The term would seem to indicate a state of *insensibility*, and therefore, of freedom from distress. And yet, it is a *painful hardness of heart;* it is a *distressing insensibility.* The subjects of it, generally think themselves void of feelings, and write bitter things against themselves on account of it. But still their hearts are feeling most exquisitely. What is called hardness of heart, is not want of feelings; but want of those particular feelings, which are enjoyed when religion prospers in the soul. The heart is insensible to those considerations which used to wake it into glowing holy exercises. Yet, this heart may, at the same time, be deeply distressed on this account.

Hardness of heart is *mysterious*, as well as apparently *paradoxical.* In this state of heart, saints find they cannot approach unto God with the same delight and ardour as before; yet, cannot see why. They are not alive to duty as before; and yet cannot see why. Why this deathlike languor is brooding over them, seems most unaccountable.

At such times, too, they are harrassed with what is called *unbelief.* They can neither appropriate nor appreciate the promises as in times past. Yet, they believe these promises to be true and precious. But they do not *feel* their truth and preciousness.

But why they cannot, is unaccountable. This perplexes or distresses them; and they cry out, "Lord, I believe; help thou mine unbelief." Mark ix. 24.

Sometimes, spiritual darkness is attended with violent temptations. Satan suggests to saints such blasphemous thoughts, and such wicked purposes, as are abhorrent to them. And fearing, lest these wicked thoughts are the workings of their own hearts, they are filled with anguish on account of them. Bunyan says of his pilgrim, as he passed through the *valley of the shadow of death*, "I took notice that now poor Christian was so confounded, that he did not know his own voice; and thus I perceived it; just when he was come over against the mouth of the burning pit, one of the wicked ones got behind him, and stepped up softly to him, and whisperingly suggested many grievous blasphemies to him, which he verily thought had proceeded from his own mind. This put Christian more to it than any thing that he met with before, even to think that he should now blaspheme him that he loved so much before; yet, if he could have helped it, he would not have done it: but he had not the discretion either to stop his ears, or to know from whence those blasphemies came."

And in spiritual darkness, there is a loss of that enjoyment which is felt in the full exercise of love, gratitude, zeal, and other holy affections. This loss occasions painful regret. In this darkness, there is a hungering and thirsting after righteousness, which for the time, is not satisfied. This, also, is painful. In this darkness, saints feel deeply condemned for their want of ardent love to God, trust in his dealings, and zeal in his cause. And all these things combined, make it a most distressing state.

Spiritual darkness has doubtless its benefits. It leads the saint to a fuller acquaintance with himself, and with the devices of Satan; causes him to feel his own weakness more fully; to see his need of continual assistance of grace; to look for it more constantly, and to prize it more highly. It serves to test his faith, and show him whether it be genuine. It serves also, to purify and strengthen it. Hence, says the apostle, "Wherein ye greatly rejoice, though now for a season, (if *need be*,) ye are in heaviness through manifold temptations: that the trial of your faith being much more precious than of gold that perisheth, though it be tried with fire, might be found unto praise, and honour, and glory, at the appearing of Jesus Christ." 1 Pet. i. 6, 7. And says another apostle, "My brethren, count it all joy when ye fall into divers temptations; knowing this, that the trying of your faith worketh patience. But let patience have her perfect work, that ye may be perfect and entire, wanting nothing." James i. 2—4. And spiritual darkness is an affliction. But numerous are the promises of Scripture, that afflictions shall work together for the good of the afflicted saint. Nay, he has promises, that it shall work out for him, "a far more exceeding and eternal weight of glory." 2 Cor. iv. 17.

Still, however, in itself considered, this darkness is an evil to be dreaded and avoided. Instead of running into it, we should pray, "Lead us not into temptation, but deliver us from evil." And whenever we are afflicted with such darkness, we should strive to escape from it as soon as possible.

But God alone, can grant the needed deliverance. The saint in darkness, should therefore cry out to God, like the Psalmist, " I have gone astray like a lost sheep; seek thy servant; for I do not forget thy commandments." Ps. cxix. 176. And when he is restored to the light, he must say, " Thanks be to God, who giveth us the victory through our Lord Jesus Christ." 1 Cor. xv. 57.

Sometimes the manifestation is sudden and powerful. Although a heavy and impervious gloom has long settled around the saint, the cloud is at once dispelled, and the sun of righteousness shines suddenly, and in full effulgence, on his soul. But generally, the light returns by slow degrees, like the dawning of the morning light, or the gradual melting away of the clouds, that have long enveloped the sky. Yet, let the light come as it may, it is evidently the result of divine and sovereign mercy.

But, although relief from this darkness comes from God's sovereign grace, still there is something, yea, much to be done, by him who would receive it. It is with this, as with saving grace. Salvation comes from God only. Yet, the sinner is to seek it in certain ways of God's appointment. So, there are certain things which saints in darkness are to do, as the means of obtaining the sovereign relief which God alone can give. Indeed, God never brings the saint out of darkness, till he brings him out of that stupid and negligent state that has caused his darkness. To do this, he often employs *means* upon him; and most frequently, does he bring him back by some temporal affliction, such as the loss of property, loss of friends, sickness, disappointments, or other sore calamities. And the distress of spiritual darkness, is itself an affliction, and is evidently intended to rouse up the saint from his lukewarm or backslidden state. It is not to be expected, then, that his darkness will disperse, so long as he remains inactive. He has something then to do, before he can reasonably expect that light will arise to him.

DIRECTIONS TO SAINTS IN SPIRITUAL DARKNESS.

1. *Consider the nature of your mental depression.* All dejection of mind, is not spiritual darkness. The unregenerate have *their* melancholy hours. And the same causes will produce the like effects upon the Christian. When the melancholy emotions produced by these natural causes have place in the mind of a Christian, they come in contact with religion, and thereby assume a religious hue. Yet, properly they make no part of spiritual darkness. It is important, therefore, to learn the nature of your affections, that if they are of this kind, you may lay them out of your account. If you find that all your distress is of this kind, your inquiry "how you shall escape from spiritual darkness," should be at an end. You have no such darkness to escape. It is nothing but a depression of animal spirits.

But it may be, that along with this heaviness of animal feelings, you have other affections, which constitute real spiritual darkness. And if this is the case, it is especially necessary that you discriminate your feelings, to know which are animal, and which are spiritual; that you withdraw your attention from the former, as making no part of your inquiry, and fasten your mind entirely on the latter.

If your darkness is attended (as it generally is) with doubts whether you have been born again, inquire whether your distress is that of the *awakened sinner*, or that of the *deserted saint*. If you have distinct recollection of your conviction and conversion, consider whether your present distress is like that which you endured before your supposed change of heart took place. If it be like the pains of conviction, you have but little reason to hope yourself a Christian. If it be entirely different, you may be encouraged. But inquire, farther, whether sin and holiness appear to you now, as they did before you thought you passed from death unto life? whether your distress is *dread of punishment*, or *grief at sin*? whether it is occasioned by a dread of God's future approach in judgment, or by his hiding from you the present light of his countenance? whether you *fear* his presence, or really *desire* it? For, if the former of these alternatives be true, your case looks dark indeed. But if, on the contrary, you find sin and holiness look different from what they did before conversion; if you find it is the guilt of the one, and the want of the other, that grieve you; that you are distressed more by the fact, that God withdraws the light of his countenance from you, than by the fear that he will finally draw nigh unto you to judgment; that instead of dreading, you *desire* his presence; then you may comfort yourselves with a cheering hope, that you have 'passed from death unto life.'

If your darkness is attended with what are called *hardness of heart*, and *unbelief*, consider whether this darkness be *welcome?* If it be, you may well fear, lest you are yet 'in the gall of bitterness, and bonds of iniquity.' But if, on the contrary, this hardness of heart is grievous and distressing to you, this fact is a cheering evidence that you have experienced a saving change of heart. This distress is but a godly sorrow for sin, shaped by your present circumstances. And in all your efforts to overcome this hardness of heart, you are but sustaining that Christian warfare, which none but the Christian ever wages. Inquire, then, whether there be not a conflict within, of which the apostle speaks, when he says, "For the flesh lusteth against the spirit, and the spirit against the flesh; and these are contrary, one to the other; so that ye cannot do the things that ye would," Gal. v. 17, and which he tells us, in the 7th chapter of Romans, he himself has felt. "For the good that I would, I do not: but the evil which I would not, that I do.—I find then a law, that when I would do good, evil is present with me. For I delight in the law of God, after the inward man: but I see another law in my members, warring against the law of my mind, and bringing me into captivity to the law of sin, which is in my members." And under the burden of this conflict, do you not cry out with him, "O wretched man that I am! who shall deliver me from the body of this death?"

You complain of your want of love to Christ.—But would you desire it, if you had never had a taste of it? You are distressed that you have no sweet communion with your God. Yet, what but grace has given you a relish for this communion? You complain that you are shut up in darkness.—But would this be distressing to you, if you had never seen the light? You complain that you have no feelings. But have you not very *distressing* feelings? And although they are not the feelings of the Christian in the *full* and *vigorous* exercises of grace, are they not still such feelings as the unregenerate never experience?

If then, these are the feelings that distress you, instead of being evidences against you, they furnish proof in favour of your saving change of heart. Instead, then, of giving way to your despondency, like the Psalmist you should chide it, saying,—"Why art thou cast down, O my soul? and why art thou disquieted within me? hope thou in God; for I shall yet praise him for the help of his countenance." Ps. xlii. 5. Call to recollection the promise of God, that though "weeping may endure for a night, joy cometh in the morning." Ps. xxx. 5. Obey the encouraging call of God: "Who is among you that feareth the Lord, that obeyeth the voice of his Servant, that walketh in darkness, and hath no light? let him trust in the name of the Lord, and stay upon his God." Isa. L. 10. And resolve with the prophet, "Although the fig-tree shall not blossom, neither shall fruit be in the vines; the labour of the olive shall fail, and the fields shall yield no meat; the flocks shall be cut off from the fold, and there shall be no herd in the stalls: yet I will rejoice in the Lord, I will joy in the God of my salvation." Hab. iii. 17, 18.

But spiritual darkness is often attended with fierce and foul temptations. And in the obscurity and commotion which takes place in the soul under the influence of this deep darkness, and of these powerful temptations, the saint often mistakes these awful insinuations of Satan, for the feelings and purposes of his own heart: and thus he brings upon himself a vast burden of groundless fear, and needless anguish. He thinks that if he were a Christian, he could not have such impious and blasphemous thoughts arise in his mind. He is, therefore, led not only into doubt, but also to the borders of despair. If such is your situation, consider whether these awful thoughts, which find their way into your mind, are welcome to your heart; or whether you view them with grief and abhorrence? If the former, you have reason to be alarmed. But if the latter, there is nothing in your case that should lead you to doubts and fears. On the contrary, your abhorrence of these wicked thoughts, is a proof that you are a subject of saving grace. If you were an unrenewed sinner, these foul thoughts would not be displeasing to you; or if any pain should be occasioned by them, it would be dread of their punishment, not hatred to their nature. It can be nothing but grace, then, that makes you look on these temptations with grief and horror. Instead of supposing that you suffer what others do not, you should consider, that all saints suffer the same *kind*, and many suffer to the same *degree* of temptations. And instead of yielding through despair of overcoming them, you should be encouraged by the word of God to expect assistance. He says, "There hath no temptation taken you, but such as is common to man: but God is faithful, who will not suffer you to be tempted above that ye are able; but will with the temptation also make a way to escape; that ye may be able to bear it." 1 Cor. x. 13.

2. *Consider the cause of your darkness.* While the cause continues, the effect will continue. You cannot, therefore, expect that your darkness will be removed, until that is removed which produces it. It is on this account important, that you search out the cause.

Some people are constitutionally gloomy. They are prone to look on the dark side of every thing; consequently, on the dark side of their spiritual concerns. With such, *native temperament* is the cause, either in part or in full. And if you find this the case with you, you must make proper allowance for that temperament, and guard against its future influence.

Ill health is often a cause of this darkness. It aggravates the gloomy temperament, where it is native; and produces it for a time, in those in whom it is not constitutional. Disease in the nerves, has especially this tendency. The hypochondria is generally supposed to exist in few forms, and those in such extreme degrees, as to render those cases very clear and striking; but it assumes a multiplicity of forms, and exists in a multiplicity of different degrees. It has influence on more minds, therefore, and to a greater extent, than is generally supposed. Probably, by far the greater part who labour under religious melancholy, are more or less affected by this disease. Persons afflicted with it, are very hard to be convinced of it. The nature of the disease is such, that the more they are afflicted by it, and therefore the more discoverable it is to another, the less are they convinced of it. But it is very important that they should be convinced of it; so that they may be comforted at finding their distress is not occasioned by the frown of God on their sins, but by the influence of disease on the mind; that they may muster fortitude to bear up against this influence. And especially is it important, in order that, by attention to their health, they may remove the cause of it.

But such persons are very unwilling to ascribe their darkness to the state of their health. They are afraid they shall ascribe to disease what arises from depravity; and thus call that their calamity, which is their sin. But where this darkness does arise from disease, it should be seen and resisted. And by refusing to do so, such persons are in danger of doing injury to themselves, and thus of committing no little sin.

But there are other approximate causes of spiritual darkness; and *neglect of duty* is generally the principal one. Often this heaviness of soul is first occasioned by the neglect of some *individual* duty.

In such case, the most effectual way to regain the light, is to return to that particular duty.—Greater attention to other duties, is not the thing necessary. If the neglect of family prayer was the cause of darkness, a greater attention to secret prayer will not answer. In this case, family prayer is the subject of demand and refusal between God and the depressed saints. For neglect of this he withdrew the light of his countenance; nor can they reasonably expect he will return it, until the point is yielded by their discharge of this duty. The same may be said of every other duty, the neglect of which, and every sin the commission of which, has caused the darkness of the soul. The most probable place where the lost comfort will be found, is the very place in which it was lost. To that place, then, it is important to repair. If you have lost your spiritual light, you must go back to that state of faithfulness, where you last enjoyed it. If you lost it by running into a particular sin, that sin must be forsaken; if by engaging in a certain employment, that employment must be relinquished; if by frequenting certain company, that company must be shunned; if by indulging in certain amusements, those amusements must be forsaken, would you enjoy again the light of God's countenance.

But we shall have occasion to speak more of the cause of darkness, in other places.

3. *Look back on past experience, and consider what were your exercises at the times when you thought you enjoyed spiritual light.* I am aware, that this measure is condemned by many. They

say, 'We can have no evidence of grace, but from present experience.' But in my opinion, this contradicts Scripture, common sense, and experience. Said Jeremiah, Lam. iii. 21, "This I recall to my mind, therefore I have hope." Here, if I rightly understand the connexion of the passage, the prophet declares, that in times of darkness, he called to mind his past experience; and this gave him hope. But, be this as it may, in many places in Scripture, we can gather from the scope of what saints have said in darkness, that they looked back to past experience. See Job xxix. Ps. xxxviii. 42—51; especially, lxiii. 2. See also Heb. x. 32, and Rev. ii. 5.—iii. 3. It is contrary to common sense. How much of our knowledge is *recollected* knowledge. The mathematician knows that *the three angles of a triangle, are equal to two right angles;* though he cannot at once glance over the whole process by which that proposition is demonstrated: he knows it, because he fully recollects that he saw the demonstration, and assuredly knew it to be correct. So of many other propositions. Indeed, if we could not know things by recollection, it would be impossible to progress in any science whatever. We can, then, know a truth, by a recollection that we have seen it proven. We can know, therefore, that we are Christians, by calling to mind our former affections—affections which are sure evidences of grace. And this accords to the experience and practice of saints in general; nay, I will venture to say, it accords with the experience and practice, even of those who object to looking back on past exercises. How do they make up their judgment respecting their state? Is it from what they *now* feel? or what they have felt in general, since they passed from death unto life?—Generally speaking, we must judge of our exercises after they are gone, or not at all. We see then, that this sentiment is contrary to Scripture, common sense, and experience.

It is true, we should advert to experience long past, with much caution; for we may have been mistaken in these affections, at the time that we had them; and now that they are passed by, we shall be still more liable to misjudge respecting them.—We should not place much reliance on them, unless we pretty clearly recollect, what was their distinctive nature. Present holy exercises are, therefore, the most satisfactory. But sometimes the saint is in such a state of mind, by reason of temptations and darkness, that he sees no present exercises to support his hope; and if he may not look to the past, it would seem that he must sink into despair. In such a condition, it is his privilege and duty, to turn his attention from the present to the past. Especially ought this to be done by those who are verging to despair. They stand most in need of it: and they will be least in danger of being led astray by means of it.*

4. *Engage much in religious meditation.* In that coldness in religion, which generally precedes

* "I have read of one who was kept from destroying himself, being much tempted by Satan thereunto, by remembering that there was a time when he solemnly set himself in prayer and self-examination before the Lord, and made a diligent inquiry into his spiritual condition; and in the close of that work, it was evidenced to him that his heart was upright with God: and this kept him from laying violent hands on himself."—*Brooks on Assurance.*

spiritual darkness, and in some of this darkness itself, there is a great wandering of the thoughts from God. This want of meditation on divine things, is one cause, then, of spiritual darkness.—This cause should therefore be removed.

But attention to religious meditation, does more than to remove this cause of spiritual darkness. It exerts a direct and positive agency in removing the darkness itself. Our thoughts naturally enkindle our feelings. "While I was musing, the fire burned." Ps. xxxix. 3. Attempts to turn the thoughts into a devotional channel, tend to stir up devout affections. Meditation excites to duty. "I thought on my ways, and turned my feet unto thy testimonies. Ps. cxix. 59. And it is evident, that when we put forth ardent holy exercises, and faithfully discharge our outward duties, there will be an end to our spiritual darkness.

If your darkness is clearly occasioned by stupidity or neglect of duty, think much on the guilt of your course. What ingratitude to the Giver of your mercies! What rash contempt of his infinite majesty! Think much on the contempt you show to his grace, and to the enjoyment to be had in faithfully serving him. Meditate much on the misery of your present state; how cheerless it is; and how very important it is that you escape from it. If you are not sufficiently alive to your lamentable situation, these meditations will serve to arouse you.

But sometimes the saint is overborne and discouraged by his doubts and fears. If this be your case, you should turn your attention away from the dark spots in the picture, and meditate on those things which are best calculated to inspire hope.—Indeed, if the heart is sunken very low in despondency, it is sometimes advisable to turn the attention away from self altogether; and resolve to seek God's glory, and the welfare of Zion, let what will become of us. Could the saint in darkness come to this resolution, he would not keep it long, before the light would return.

5. *Converse freely with pious and experienced friends, respecting your state.* It is hurtful to the interests of Zion, to be continually proclaiming our coldness and distress. Especially, to do it as we fear many do, out of mock humility. It is particularly hurtful, to speak of them in common social meetings; as it strikes a chill upon all saints who hear it. It has a tendency to discourage others, and to damp their ardour in the cause of Christ. If, then, you are in darkness, take heed how you injure others, by speaking of it. But in your private interviews with your minister, or pious friends, you may safely speak of your case.

Great good often results from a disclosure of the feelings under darkness. Many a one has lost a great portion of his burden, at the very moment that he began to break his mind to his friends.—We are so constituted by our benevolent Creator, that expressing our sorrows, tends to relieve us.—And so it often happens in a remarkable manner, respecting the darkness and distress of the saint.—By conversing with his pious friends on his feelings, he insensibly grows animated, and encouraged even by his own conversation, much more is he encouraged by their soothing and animating exhortations: by these friends, too, he is taught what to do to escape from his darkness, and effecually excited to make the needful efforts. And by conversing with these friends, he excites their earnest, probably, their *effectual* prayers, for his relief.

But many saints in darkness, are very unwilling to let their condition be known to their fellow saints. Either, they have such foul temptations that they are afraid to tell them to others, or they are borne down with that sullen, silent gloom, which inclines the afflicted to keep all their trouble to themselves. And yet these are the ones whose free conversation on the exercises of their mind, will do the most good. Tempted saints are apt to suppose that other saints experience no such trials. But by making them known to their brethren, they find that these are no uncommon trials, among the followers of Christ. Their brethren tell them they have felt the same. They tell them, "There hath no temptation taken you, but such as is common to man; but God is faithful, who will not suffer you to be tempted, above that ye are able; but will, with the temptation, also make a way to escape, that ye may be able to bear it." 1 Cor. x. 13.—And no means are so apt to dispel the clouds of silent, sullen grief, as conversing freely on the subject. In spiritual darkness, fail not, then, to consult your pious friends, respecting your spiritual sorrows.

6. *Read with great attention such books as relate to spiritual darkness.* Many books that treat on experimental religion, especially such as treat

on the evidences of grace, may be read with great profit. But the book which should have your chief attention, is *the word of God.* Read it not occasionally, and with long intervals, but read it constantly: read it not in a hurried and careless manner; but with an earnest endeavour to understand its meaning; especially, to understand what it says in relation to the trials and distresses of the saints. But spend not your time in poring over the difficult and mysterious doctrines. Important as these doctrines are in themselves, and much as you ought to study them, this is not your time for it. If in your heaviness of spirit, you attempt to study upon them, your distress will probably increase. And the understanding of these abstruse doctrines, is not necessary to your salvation, much less to your deliverance from spiritual darkness. And while thus distressed, your minds are in a state most unsuited to the investigation of what is "hard to be understood." In consulting the word of God, you should therefore turn from these doctrines to the direct precepts of God's law, to his offers of salvation, and to the evidences of saving grace. But the *devotional* parts of Scripture, are still better suited to your condition; for they are better suited to awake those devotional feelings, which you more especially need, in order to dispel the darkness that surrounds you. The Psalms are peculiarly suited to your case. They are not only devotional, but in many places, are very expressive of the various feelings of saints in darkness, and point them to their duty in respect to it. This is somewhat the case with Isaiah, Jeremiah, Lamentations, and some of the minor prophets. The same may be said of John xiv. Romans vii. 1 Peter i. Heb. xii. and indeed many other portions of the New Testament, which point out the trials and troubles that saints endure. Whenever you read the Scriptures promiscuously, or by course, be continually looking out for some portions, that have a bearing on your case; and when you find them, read them repeatedly, and with peculiar endeavours to gain their full meaning; and make a proper improvement of them.

7. *Keep as much as possible from worldly concerns and temptations.* These are often the cause of the saint's darkness. It often happens, that by overwhelming himself in worldly cares, associating with wicked companions; following worldly pleasures; engaging in employments, or going to places, which expose to temptation; he is led away from duty, and finally away from light and comfort. In such cases, the first thing is, to remove the *cause;* which is, to forsake these worldly cares, or these exposures to temptation.

But if the darkness were not occasioned by these things, still it is important to keep away from them; for they have no small influence in preventing the light of the Sun of righteousness from returning to the soul. Many that are in deep darkness, would probably rise at once to those vigorous affections, and that faithful obedience, which secure hope and comfort in the Lord, if they were not kept down by incumbering cares, embarrassing connexions, or other exposures to strong temptations. If their condition in life is such, that they cannot free themselves from these things, we may hope that God will extend them special relief. But if, while they might free themselves from these cares, and might forsake these occasions of temptations, they neglect to do so, their prospect looks dark indeed. It is true, they *might* rise, notwithstanding all these burdens; yet there is little hope that they *will.*—But if they would at once break away from them, they might find the way to the light of God's countenance, with far less difficulty. And this act of self-denial, in tearing away from them, would meet the favour of God, and call down upon them the enlightening influence of the Spirit of God.

If, then, you wish deliverance from your darkness, be careful not to be burdened or perplexed with worldly cares. Be very careful not to undertake to do more in a given time, than you can easily perform; for it will crowd off your attention from holy things, while striving to accomplish it. And if you fail to accomplish it, the failure will vex you, and thus carry you still farther from God.

If you must have cares, be careful not to be perplexed with them. Let them not disturb and ruffle your mind. Keep it continually in mind, that these cares are of immensely less importance than the concerns of the soul. And be especially careful, not to let your desire of gain engross your attention; for remember, "They that *will* be rich, fall into temptation and a snare, and into many foolish and hurtful lusts, which drown men in destruction and perdition. For the love of money, is the root of all evil: *which, while some coveted af-*

ter, they have erred from the faith, and pierced themselves through with many sorrows." 1 Tim. vi. 9, 10.

8. *Be very constant and exact in outward duties.* And to this, I would call your special attention. Neglect of outward duties, is almost invariably the principal cause of spiritual darkness. It is, therefore, of vast importance, by returning to obedience, to remove this cause. And this return to obedience, will not only remove the cause of darkness; but will have a direct and positive influence, in recalling light and comfort. Obedience is calculated to quicken the saint in his Christian course; and thus to animate and comfort him. And obedience secures the favour of God; and thus ensures that grace which gives light and peace. The light of Heaven always shines on the narrow path of righteousness. Said Christ, "He that followeth me," [that is, in the way of faithful obedience,] "shall not walk in darkness, but shall have the light of life." St. John viii. 12.

Yet when the Christian gets into darkness, he generally grows more negligent in outward duties. At such times, his zeal, love, faith, patience, and other graces, are generally very faint. This renders outward duties painful, and inclines him to neglect them. And through the influence of Satan's devices, he is led to think he *ought* to neglect them. He is led to think that outward duties, done with such faint affections as he has, must be vain formalities, which God abhors; and therefore, he had better omit than perform them. Nay, as in this state of darkness, it is doubtful whether he is a Christian, he is led to think it will be nothing but hypocrisy for him to attempt doing outward good works.

But such a course of reasoning, is very incorrect and dangerous. Why should he neglect his outward duties? For fear of heartless formality?—What is that formality which God condemns? It is doing outward duties with a design to satisfy the claims of God with the mere external performance. But the outward obedience of the saint in darkness, is not of this nature. So far is *he* from attempting to satisfy God with it, that he is dissatisfied with it himself. He mourns that his outward obedience is not attended with its correspondent and ardent affections. Outward duties, performed in such circumstances, instead of being offensive formality, is the practice of self-denial; and is the waging of that spiritual warfare which God commands. It must, therefore, be acceptable to him. Especially, must it be *less* offensive to him, than the utter neglect of duty. What! Would God be more displeased with him for *trying* to do his duty, than for *utterly neglecting* it? These very outward duties are commanded. They are right in themselves. They ought, therefore, to be done. No want of corresponding affections of the heart are any excuse for omitting them. Because the *heart* is not right in its *feelings*, is that any reason why the *hand* should not be right in its *doings*? Outward obedience is the duty of the saint, just as much when he is in darkness, as when he is in the light. And it is a poor servant that will work only when the sun shines. It is a poor soldier that will fight only when he sees the position and strength of the enemy, and has assurance of victory.

Equally vain is it to neglect outward obedience for fear of *hypocrisy*. Can that be hypocrisy which the saint performs in this state of mind? When he tries to do his duty, and on finding he comes short of it, acknowledges it, and mourns over it, will God frown upon him for hypocrisy? Will he not rather frown upon him because he directly refuses to do what is directly commanded, and what is evidently due from him to his Maker? Instead of refusing to discharge outward duties, because he is in darkness, he should rather resolve to do all in his power for the glory of God, whether he be saved or lost.

But our subject leads us to consider, not so much what is *right*, as what is *profitable* to you in darkness. In regard to your interest, why should you neglect outward obedience? This will give you no relief. On the contrary, it will tend to increase your distress. Are you cold and stupid now? If you leave off outward duties, you will be still more so. Low as you now are, the outward obedience to which you have attended has kept you from sinking still lower. No, instead of omitting it, you should be more constant and strict than ever in it. In a time of spiritual darkness, instead of being more lax, you need to be much more punctual than ever. For outward obedience has influence upon the internal exercises. Neglect of it, chills the heart. Faithful attention to it, serves to warm and invigorate the heart. If, then, for a while you will be very constant and strict in every outward duty, you will find a change in your feelings. Your light and enjoyment will soon return.

Here lies your chief difficulty, in relation to spiritual darkness. Just so soon as you get away into darkness, just so soon you grow lax in outward duties; and the farther you get into the dark, the more you neglect these duties. And thus, by your own conduct, you thicken the gloom. Whereas, did you keep on in the constant, undeviating course of outward obedience, there would be little to fear. Your distress would be light, and not of long continuance. You should meet a season of darkness, just as a traveller meets a heavy squall of snow: You should get your course before the darkness comes on: and in the darkness you should keep on in that course, though like the traveller, you scarcely see where you are treading. When the cloud is gone by, and the light is returned, you will find that, like the traveller, you have all the while been making progress; that you have come out of the cloud the sooner on that account; and that on the same account, you are farther advanced in your Christian course. In all your darkness, then, be very precise in the discharge of outward duties.—Be very cautious how Satan tempts you away from it. He is very anxious to do so, because punctual discharge of duty most effectually secures you against darkness and distress; while neglect of it, is obedience to him, promotes his cause, and leads you to that deep darkness which he would have you endure.

But there is one outward duty which probably you will be more tempted to neglect than all others.

That is, *coming to the sacrament of the Lord's supper.* You will be liable to think that as you are so cold in religion, if not wholly destitute of it, you have no right to approach the table of the Lord; and thus you will be apt to keep back. But consider, that though you have no right to come in a wrong state of mind, you have no right to stay away. The commemoration of a Saviour's death, is a *duty;* a duty which you have no right to neglect. It is, moreover, a duty which *you* have vowed to God, and promised to your brethren to perform. You are, therefore, under double obligation to attend to it. If, then, you withdraw from so important a duty, you must expect God will manifest his displeasure at you in the greater desertion and darkness.

The Lord's supper is an ordinance more particularly designed for the comfort of saints. It is an ordinance in which God more frequently sheds peculiar light upon his people. To neglect this ordinance, is more directly provoking God to keep you in darkness. If, then, you are in great heaviness, it is more especially necessary that you attend on this sacred ordinance. Many a one has gone with great discouragement and darkness to it; but while receiving the tokens of a Saviour's love, have received peculiar light and comfort. "Go and do likewise," that you may receive the same relief.

Lastly, *Be much at the throne of grace.* This is, indeed, an outward duty, and might have been considered under the foregoing head. But it is so important, that it deserves a separate attention.—Neglect of prayer, is often the principal cause of darkness. Sometimes it is the neglect of *family prayer*, but more frequently the neglect of *secret prayer*, that occasions it. This cause must be removed, by returning to the neglected duties. To continue neglecting prayer, will be to continue causing darkness. If you return not to the throne of grace, then you must expect the gloom to thicken.

But prayer not only prevents greater darkness, but promotes spiritual light. The discharge of duty *in general*, has a tendency to wake up the heart to more energy. But the duty of prayer has much the most powerful tendency. In prayer, you confess your sins, and seek the pardon of them.—This has a tendency to awake you to penitence for them. In prayer, you recount your sorrows; and this has a tendency to awake you to more earnest desire and vigorous exertions for deliverance:—And in prayer, you acknowledge your obligations to God; and this will have a tendency to awake a more earnest desire to discharge them.

We are, moreover, taught to pray for deliverance from darkness, and to expect that deliverance, in answer to our prayers. Said the Psalmist, "I have gone astray like a lost sheep: *seek thy servant*, for I do not forget thy commandments." Ps. cxix. 176. If ever you are delivered from your darkness, your deliverance must be effected by God's sovereign grace; and that grace is given in answer to prayer.

But prayer is a duty which the saint in darkness finds very difficult to perform. Generally his thoughts wander, and it is difficult to confine them to prayer: his affections are languid, and it is difficult to arouse them to devotion. This inclines him to neglect it. This, and Satan's temptations, lead him to think he may as well not pray at all, as pray in so cold and formal a manner. But so sure as he gives way to these things, he sinks into deeper darkness. You must strive, therefore, to control these mental wanderings; you must strive to rouse up these drowsy affections. This you can do: Resolution and energy will soon accomplish it, and render prayer again easy and delightful.—And when this is done, the darkness is gone. It is important, therefore, that you pray *more* in darkness, than in times of light and comfort. You should especially be cautious at no time to neglect it through discouragement. You may find relief (as many others have) when you least expect it.—And if ever you find it, probably it will be at the throne of grace. Say not you have no spirit of prayer, and therefore it will be of no use to attempt to pray; for the mercy-seat is the very place to find the spirit.

As prayer is so effectual in recalling the light of God's countenance, it is very important that you make vigorous exertions to rouse yourselves up to it. The more vigorous these exertions are, the more efficacious they will be; and the more speedily will the object be accomplished. It is, therefore, expedient that you set apart a day of *fasting, humiliation and prayer.* And it would be better still, to *go into the closet, resolved not to come out of it till you had obtained light and comfort.* Such a resolution put into faithful execution, would never fail to dispel the clouds of spiritual darkness.—

The truth of this has often been proved by experience; and this should encourage you to "Go and do likewise."

You will see, then, that when you are in spiritual darkness, instead of sitting down in indolent discouragement, you should be up and active.—You see, that instead of waiting in disobedient dleness for God to come and scatter the cloud that surrounds you, you should make diligent, and vigorous, and persevering exertions to rush from the midst of it. You see that you need to bestow much attention on the *nature* and *cause* of your darkness; you need to *look back on your past experience;* you need to *engage much in religious meditations;* you need to *converse much with pious friends respecting your case;* you need to *read much on the subject;* you need to be *very cautious to keep from worldly care and temptations;* you need to be very *constant and exact in outward duties,* and *especially to be much in prayer.*

I would add, that what you do should be done *quickly*, and *resolutely*, and *perseveringly*. The longer you delay to arise, the deeper will your darkness become; the greater will be your reluctance to employ the necessary means to dispel it, and the more obstinate will your difficulty become. The sooner you arise, the sooner will you obtain relief, and the less effort you will have to make for obtaining it. What you do, do *resolutely*. By a half determination, and a faint and fickle endeavour, you will effect nothing. To succeed, you must be firm in your determination, and vigorous in your endeavours to obtain relief. What you do, do *perseveringly*. If you give back after striving for a while, you lose all you have done; when, perhaps, but a little longer continuance would have brought success. Never think of relaxing your exertions, till you are in the full enjoyment of the light of God's countenance.

HAVING said so much for the purpose of assisting the saint to escape from spiritual darkness, it seems proper before closing the subject, to say a few words for his direction after he has escaped.—And this seems the more necessary, because he will still be liable to run into darkness again.

When once you have been delivered from this darkness, you will be liable to think you shall never be in danger of wandering into it again; and this very persuasion is what will most expose you to it. Keep it, then, in mind, that there is danger; and therefore that you need to be on guard against it. Remember, too, how painful this darkness has been to you; and let the recollection set you on the more faithful watchfulness. Consider, too, how much easier it is to get into darkness, than to get out again. The former is all the way down hill; and you slide into it by your own weight: nay, you need exertion to keep from doing so. But the latter is all up hill, steep and difficult, and requires most laborious exertions to regain your standing. It is much easier to *keep* out, than to *get* out of this distressing state.

It will not be expedient here, to enumerate the several means which should be employed for keeping the soul from spiritual darkness. It may be said with few exceptions, that those means which *restore* the light, are the best for *retaining* it. In other words, whatever keeps us in the vigorous exercise of holy affections, and the faithful discharge of Christian duty, will secure us against spiritual darkness. God grant that the reader and the writer may be constantly faithful in duty, and thus secure the continued light of the Sun of righteousness.

www.ingramcontent.com/pod-product-compliance
Lightning Source LLC
LaVergne TN
LVHW021406110826
845150LV00007B/1807